PRAISE FOR **WHOLE GIRL**

"I have had the privilege and pleasure of being uplifted by Sadie's cooking and outlook on life over the past few years. Her outlooks on food, the teenage experience, and where our healthiest emotional priorities lie are so refreshing and comforting in these troubled times when teens are up against so much terrible coercion to feel as though they aren't good enough. Sadie has set out on a journey to feed their stomachs and their minds with her beautiful attitude and respect for all women everywhere. I'm glad she came into my life, and I hope she nourishes yours as she has mine. She's a true role model."

Jameela Jamil

actress (*The Good Place*), activist, and founder of I Weigh

"In a world full of folks with remarkable talent, every once in a while a literal star emerges . . . and by star I mean a beacon of inspiration, insight, and hope. Sadie Radinsky is at once beacon, star, and hope. She has tackled the tough topic of helping her peers come to a better place with themselves and building a better understanding of food. *Whole Girl* is an amazing resource for anyone, but it is critical reading for young women looking for healthy ways to navigate their lives, emotions, and our complex food world."

Robb Wolf

New York Times bestselling author of *The Paleo Solution* and *Wired to Eat*

"Sadie's book reads like a long, heartwarming, and uplifting conversation with a new friend—one you walk away from knowing yourself a little better. I'm so excited for young people to pick up this book, explore the world through new eyes, and forge an exploratory relationship with nourishment, both through her fantastic recipes and the journey of self-knowledge."

Stephanie Beatriz

actress (*Brooklyn Nine-Nine, In the Heights*)

"*Whole Girl* nourishes body, mind, and soul. In a world where food is commonly geared towards weight loss for young girls, Sadie created a book with no concept of 'loss' but rather what one can gain from a joyful, creative, and positive relationship with food."

Jade Pettyjohn

actress (*Little Fires Everywhere, School of Rock*)

"Sadie is an inspiration to all young women. Her work inspires all of us to take better care of ourselves and truly embrace a healthy relationship with food."

Kelly LeVeque

nutritionist and author of *Body Love* and *Body Love Every Day*

"Sadie wrote *Whole Girl* in a down-to-earth and authentic tone that makes it such a fun read. There's an amazing diversity of people interviewed to share their passions and lessons. After reading *Whole Girl*, I've learned how to be more mindful, listen to my gut, apply self-care tips, and be confident when handling different situations."

Mikaila Ulmer
founder and CEO of Me & the Bees Lemonade, *Time* magazine
Top 30 Most Influential Teens, and author of *Bee Fearless*

"Sadie [is] one of the most inspiring young women I have ever crossed paths with. From her incredible palate to her beautiful imagery, Sadie is a visionary."

Nikki Reed
actress (*The Twilight Saga*) and writer

"Sadie Radinsky takes a joyful—and delicious!—approach to encouraging girls and young women to care for themselves as lovingly as they tend to others."

Lisa Damour, PhD
teen girl psychology expert and *New York Times*
bestselling author of *Untangled* and *Under Pressure*

"*Whole Girl* is a book every girl, no matter what age or season of life they are in, should read. Being a celiac, as well as an actress in today's culture, I have had my own struggles with my relationship with food and self-love, and this book is the perfect balance of perspective, compassion, and real-life tools to find your most energetic, happy self. From the delicious feel-good recipes to the mindful movement exercises, I took so much away from this book. As you read, you can't help but feel how intentional and passionate Sadie is."

Brec Bassinger
actress (*Stargirl, Bella and the Bulldogs*)

"Sadie has the gumption, spunk, and awareness I wish I had at her age—or any age for that matter. She is the pinnacle of a person taking destiny into their own hands no matter what stage of life they are in, and for that, I love coming across her content. Now I am glad I have it all in one scrumptious book."

Holland Roden
actress (*Teen Wolf*)

WHOLE GIRL

WHOLE GIRL

Live vibrantly, love your entire self, and make friends with food

SADIE RADINSKY

Photographs by Kelly Radinsky
Illustrations by Sofia Szamosi

sounds true
BOULDER, COLORADO

Sounds True
Boulder, CO 80306

This book is not intended as a substitute for the medical recommendations of physicians, mental health professionals, or other health-care providers. Rather, it is intended to offer information to help the reader cooperate with physicians, mental health professionals, and health-care providers in a mutual quest for optimal well-being. We advise readers to carefully review and understand the ideas presented and to seek the advice of a qualified professional before attempting to use them.

Published 2021

Cover and book design by Linsey Dodaro
Illustrations by Sophia Szamosi
Interior photos by Kelly Radinsky
Author cover photo © Kelly Radinsky

Printed in the United States of America

Library of Congress Cataloging-in-Publication Data

Names: Radinsky, Sadie, author.
Title: Whole girl : love your entire self, live vibrantly, and make friends
  with food / Sadie Radinsky.
Description: Boulder, CO : Sounds True, [2021] | "With 60 gluten-free & Paleo
  treat recipes"--Title page. | Includes bibliographical references. |
  Audience: Grades 10-12 (provided by Sounds True.)
Identifiers: LCCN 2020007700 (print) | LCCN 2020007701 (ebook) | ISBN
  9781683645719 (ebook) | ISBN 9781683645702 (hardback) | ISBN
  9781683645702 (hardback) | ISBN 9781683645719 (ebook)
Subjects: LCSH: Self-esteem in adolescence--Juvenile literature. |
  Self-acceptance in adolescence--Juvenile literature. | Teenage
  girls--Psychology--Juvenile literature. | Teenage
  girls--Nutrition--Juvenile literature.
Classification: LCC BF724.3.S36 (ebook) | LCC BF724.3.S36 R34 2021 (print) |
  DDC 155.5/182--dc23
LC record available at https://lccn.loc.gov/2020007700

10 9 8 7 6 5 4 3 2 1

Contents

Introduction

We Are All Whole

Young women are powerful.

Our brains are bursting with creativity, intellect, and new ideas. We are eager to try new things. We care passionately about issues, from global to personal. We are all different; each of us has completely unique abilities and personalities. We are full of possibility.

All of this terrifies our society. They can't handle us, in all our messy, diverse awesomeness. So they try to break us into pieces and put us in boxes. The messages are relentless: *You're not enough. You're too much. Be quiet. Don't make waves. Smile. Don't eat too much. Don't be so emotional.*

At the same time, manufacturers, media companies, and other corporations profit off our insecurities. They make us feel bad about ourselves to get our money. *You'd be happier if you bought that. You need more followers. Buy these clothes; don't wear those.* They sell us new phones, diet products, skin-care serums, and everything else under the sun, with a side of shame.

These messages hound us so often that we start to buy into them. We actually believe we're incomplete!

But we don't need to accept this madness. We know that we're already whole.

In this book, we are going to embrace our whole selves—every part of us—*just as we are.* All the messy details. All the power and potential. We can reject society's arbitrary rules by treating ourselves with respect, enjoying food, and relishing this incredible time in life.

What Brought Me Here

The path that led me to write this book started when I was nine years old. Seemingly out of nowhere, I had developed nausea, stomachaches, and fatigue that just wouldn't go away. These symptoms kept me home and out of school for half a year (not the idyllic endless vacation it sounds like!). The worst part was that nobody could figure out what was wrong with me, including the many doctors I saw.

When my mom asked the doctors if food played a role in my issues, or if gluten could be the problem, every one of them said no. I went completely off gluten anyway, as a last resort.

Within two months, all my symptoms were gone.

I went back to school and normal (gluten-free) life. Now that I had witnessed the power of food, I started experimenting with different ways of eating. I found that I felt even better when I ate unprocessed foods and consumed less grains and sugar. I started eating more vegetables, fruits, nuts, meat, and eggs. Now I had more energy than ever before. I felt fantastic.

However, one thing was still missing from my life: desserts. Back then, decent gluten-free treats weren't available in stores. But, like they say, necessity is the mother of invention. And I needed treats. So I started inventing my own!

Every day after school, I would rush to the kitchen to concoct new cakes, muffins, and cookies. Baking grain-free desserts became my obsession. I wanted to share that joy with others. So, when I was twelve, I started posting my recipes on a blog I called *Whole Girl*. As I posted more recipes, the blog developed a following. Soon I was getting messages from people all over the world saying that my recipes had helped them. People were writing to ask me questions and share their stories. I was amazed and inspired.

On the Move

I've never been super sporty. In fact, I've never done competitive sports. Ever. But after gaining tons of energy, I wanted to move!

I began exploring different kinds of movement. I decided to try a beginner's yoga class at my local studio. I was amazed by how *strong* yoga made me feel—something I'd never really felt before. The yoga class also had a long period of meditation at the end, which made me feel calm and centered. I began going to yoga regularly and practicing yoga and meditation at home. Now every time I step onto the mat and move

through yoga—or just sit still and breathe—I get in touch with my body and grow closer to myself.

Running always perplexed me. I wondered, why do people ever run *by choice*? But after doing the dreaded Mile Run in middle-school gym class (and finishing in second-to-last place), I decided I wanted to improve. So I started running half a mile on the hiking trails near my home. Then one mile. I remember crying with frustration when I found out that it had taken me fifteen minutes to run that mile. But I kept going. I eventually worked my way up to five or six miles at a time—that is, between my many ankle sprains and knee injuries.

I tend to get hurt a lot. Every time I broke my foot (once, walking *up* stairs) or twisted my ankle, I had stop exercising in order to heal. Once I was rehabilitated, I had to start the process all over again—back to the most basic yoga poses; back to running one mile, then two. It was frustrating. I got mad at myself for being slow and weak.

But as time went by, I saw how absurd it was to be so hard on myself. I love moving my body because it clears my mind and makes me feel alive. I decided to only focus on that. I vowed not to care about how hard I exercised, or for how long or how fast. I would come from a place of patience and compassion for myself.

This new practice changed the entire way I thought about myself. I beat myself up less. I appreciated myself more.

I wanted to share this approach to exercise with other girls. So I started writing about it on my blog, along with the recipes. I talked about exercising with the motivation of being kind to myself, about learning to quiet the shaming perfectionist in me—even when I wasn't fast or strong. Apparently a lot of people struggle with the same feelings, because women and girls around the world responded, saying that my stories helped them feel less alone.

Growing Up

Meanwhile, I entered teendom. At first it was hard for me to take care of myself amid all the new stress of school and homework. So I began experimenting. I played around with different ways to help my body and mind feel good, such as preparing school lunches for the coming week and finding different ways to get more sleep. I spoke about these tools, and many more, on my website, on social media, in articles for magazines, and on my podcast.

I read messages daily from young women about their experiences with food, exercising, and taking care of themselves. I also share my own experiences and have conversations with people. It's been eye-opening to learn about other people's perspectives and to create real connections with young women around the world.

Here's the Plan

You know those emotions that society wants us to squelch? They're actually our super-powers. They give us focus, energy, compassion, strength.

In this book, we're going to rediscover our turbo-charged emotions and use them as rocket fuel to power all different parts of our lives.

Each chapter will connect us with a different mood and help us flex it in three ways:

LIVING LARGE

For each mood, we'll delve into issues young women face today, such as trying to fit in, stressing about food, not getting enough sleep, spending endless time in the abyss of our phones, and a lot more. We'll explore ways to take on these problems, using the mood from each chapter. I'll share experiences and insights that have helped in my life. We'll also hear advice from some really inspiring women I've talked with.

Each chapter will also have a Q&A. Some of the questions come directly from readers over the years. Others are composites or hypotheticals.

MINDFUL MOVEMENT

Women have been taught by our culture (and especially through advertising) that the sole purpose of exercise is to change our bodies. So working out often feels like punishment.

We're going to turn that around and approach exercise with the goal of *honoring* our bodies.

Each chapter has a mindful movement to help us tune in to each mood. If we're in a joyful state, we'll run intervals. If we're feeling cozy, we'll do gentle stretches. If we're mad, we'll use our voice with Lion's Breath.

FEED YOURSELF

For far too long, our culture has sent us messages that we should be ashamed of eating. *Eating*—something we must do to survive, and which is also the most awesome way to connect with friends and family.

We need to turn this insanity around. By fully appreciating and loving food, we can ease some of the stress and confusion surrounding it.

I believe making and eating desserts are two of the greatest joys in life. Each chapter has three recipes for incredible treats that are centered around that chapter's mood. Every recipe is gluten-free, dairy-free, and Paleo. (Many are also vegan, nut-free, and sugar-free.) Because the treats are Paleo, they have no grains or dairy, and very little sugar. They leave us feeling satisfied and energetic. No sugar crashes. And I'm not joking when I say they are yummier than conventional treats!

A Note on Gender

The title of this book and many of its ideas refer to traditional gender roles of male/female, men/women, boys/girls. Of course, humankind includes a broad spectrum of gender identities, and the issues I address in this book may apply to all different people, not just those who identify as "girls." I hope everyone feels welcome and can benefit from these chapters.

I'm thrilled to share my experiences, stories, and insights—not to mention some insane treats! Thank you for being here.

About the Recipes

Why Paleo Treats?

I am a firm believer in dessert. Dessert is delicious, but it's also special. When we share dessert with people we love, we bond and create memories. I don't recall much from when I was five, but I vividly remember the pink-and-purple castle cake my mom and I made for my birthday!

Treats have brought so much joy into my life. I want to share that joy with you. So this book is filled with forty-five treat recipes—from muffins, to cakes, to cookies, to the ultimate fudgy brownies.

Sadly, treats don't always agree with our bodies. Most are loaded with sugar, which can cause a host of serious health problems. It can also make us feel lousy. It gets us wired, then we crash. And sugar is extremely addictive. Consuming it only makes us want more and more. We can never get enough.

Most baked goods are also made with wheat—and its gluten—which causes health problems for lots of people. Gluten can mess with all different parts of the body, from the gut to the brain. Many of us are just recently learning about this connection.

With Paleo treats, we avoid these problems! *Paleo* means that all these recipes are free of grains (including gluten), dairy, legumes, and refined sweeteners. They're also low in sugar and high in protein and fat.

Speaking of fat, something needs to be said once and for all: *fat doesn't make us fat*. For decades fat has been mistakenly blamed for weight gain, heart issues, and other problems. But thanks to mounting scientific evidence, the low-fat diet myth of the last century is finally being debunked. Unfortunately, a lot of people, including many doctors, still stick to the outdated claims against fat. (If you're interested in reading about the exciting developments in science involving fat, sugar, and other food topics, see the resources section at the end of this book.)

When I started baking Paleo treats, I was amazed. They actually made me feel *good*. Eating a hunk of Paleo lemon cake made me feel energetic and also satisfied. Energetic— from cake! This is because the recipes—using ingredients such as almond flour, coconut oil, and eggs—are high in fat and protein, which fuel our bodies and leave us feeling good.

Even more surprising, Paleo treats taste delicious. They are not just similar to but better than the ones I ate in the gluten days. They're moist and fluffy, not dry. They're *flavorful*. My friends who are used to regular baked goods agree that these treats taste incredible. By comparison, the conventional treats I used to eat were actually pretty tasteless, since their flavors were masked by all the sugar. Paleo treats have very little sugar, so they open up a whole world of complex and delicious flavors.

I can't tell you how happy it makes me to share these recipes with you. Whether you're skeptical about baking without grains or you've been Paleo for years or maybe you've never baked a cake in your life, I encourage you to try these. You'll see how good a cupcake can be, and how good you can feel after eating two . . . or three!

Baking Tidbits and Tips

Baking has become one of my favorite things in life, but not for the reasons you may think. Yes, it has obvious rewards! But my favorite part is actually the process.

Getting in the kitchen and cooking up something sweet is a relaxing, almost meditative experience. It provides a calming break from my busy life. It also has become one of my favorite ways to practice self-care. It's nice when someone else cooks for us. But there's nothing more comforting than taking the time to make ourselves a batch of muffins, then eating them straight out of the oven.

Above all, baking is creative. With the right ingredients, you can bake just about anything your heart desires. So feel free to use these recipes as starting points. Get messy in the kitchen. Get covered in (almond) flour. Play with flavors. Would a sprinkle of flaky sea salt taste good here? Or a handful of walnuts add a nice crunch there? Experiment.

As you bake these recipes, or create your own, don't be hard on yourself if you totally mess up. I can't tell you how many times I've set out to make marshmallows but instead ended up crying, covered in chunks of some weird gooey substance. Okay, it was three times. But I'm learning to detach from the results of my baking; the process is what matters. So you burned your muffins. Did you have fun making them? That's all that matters!

(Plus, burned cookies can actually taste pretty good.) Let yourself mess up as much as you need to; it will only make you a better baker.

Here are some baking tips I've learned over the years. I hope they help you feel more confident jumping into the recipes that await.

- **Study your recipe.** Read through the list of ingredients and instructions before starting. Make sure you have all the ingredients and equipment on hand. There's nothing worse than realizing halfway through a recipe that you're all out of baking soda!

- **Choose the middle.** Always bake using the middle rack of your oven.

- **Preheat your oven.** Every recipe tells you when to preheat your oven. Preheat it right when the recipe says to—don't wait until later!

- **Oven temperatures vary.** A cake that needs to bake for thirty minutes in my oven may only need twenty-eight in yours. The best solution is to keep a close eye on your treats, so they don't burn. I recommend peeking through your oven window about five minutes before the recipe says to take them out. (Try not to open the oven door while the treats are baking, as it can deflate them.)

- **Double boiler DIY.** Some recipes call for a double boiler, which is a special type of pan that cooks ingredients slowly and evenly. It's easy to recreate a double boiler at home. Here's how:

  1. Fill a medium saucepan with about 1½ inches of water.
  2. Put a heatproof bowl on top of the saucepan. It shouldn't touch the water.
  3. Place the ingredients in the bowl as instructed in the recipe.
  4. Turn the stove onto medium-high heat so that the water in the saucepan boils. Cook your ingredients in the upper half as instructed.

- **Parchment paper 101.** Many recipes say to "line a baking dish with parchment paper." To do that: Tear off a large piece of parchment paper. Place your baking dish on top of the sheet. Using scissors, cut four squares off the sheet of parchment, each at the corner of the dish. Place the parchment paper inside the baking dish, so that the four flaps go up and over the sides. Trim off any extra parchment from the flaps.

- **Egg-cellent baking.** Always let your eggs sit out on the counter before baking, so they can reach room temperature. Adding cold eggs to your batter might cause some ingredients to solidify.

- **Keep clean.** If you're messy like me, always wear an apron or some old clothes!

Guide to Recipe Icons

All recipes in this book are gluten-free, grain-free, dairy-free, and refined sugar-free. Additional allergy and diet markings are as follows:

 Egg-Free.

Sugar-Free.

Vegan. Contains no animal products.

 Nut-Free. Contains no tree nuts (except for coconut, which the FDA currently defines as a tree nut).

CHAPTER ONE
Be Loving

We express love in so many different ways. A lot of the time, we put our energy into loving other people, which is awesome. But right now we're going to focus on loving ourselves. This can be really tricky! It's hard to appreciate all the different aspects of who we are—our essence—when society is obsessed with one thing: our appearance. Our culture puts so much stock in the way females look that it's hard for even us to see past it.

It's time we ditch this insanity and love the parts of us that truly matter.

The Everything Bagel

"God, you're so tall!"
—Random stranger when I was four years old. And five.
And six. And twelve. And seventeen.

It's true that I've towered over most other kids since kindergarten. But based on the way most adults talk to me, you'd think that height was the only part of me that matters.

Nearly every interaction people have with a girl is focused on one subject: her appearance. *You're so cute! Your dress is so pretty! What a nice smile!*

We don't get as many questions about our favorite books, or what we want to invent, or what our favorite song is. By a very young age, we already have the impression that our appearance is the most important aspect of who we are.

To make matters worse, we are pummeled with TV shows, ads, billboards, and an entire culture focused intensely on the way females look. It's no wonder we become hyperconscious of our appearance and spend a lot of time picking it apart.

But we are *not* the way we look. We have a million parts that make up our whole selves—the dreams we have, the people we love, the things that light us up, the way we go about the world. To love all parts of ourselves, we need to break free from our culture's crazy rules.

Jameela Jamil has a great way to do that. She is an actress, writer, DJ, radio presenter, and activist who founded the "I Weigh" movement. I Weigh invites people to post photos of themselves on social media and describe all the aspects of themselves that they're proud of—everything that *truly* defines who they are and has nothing to do with the way they look.

Thousands of people have posted using #IWeigh. Here are some of the things they "weigh":

Empathetic	Silliness	Fighter
Nerd	Dog lover	Spiritual
Curious	Extrovert	Bookworm
Evolving	Insecure	Quiet

Now it's your turn. To retrain the way you value yourself, do the I Weigh exercise. Make a list of things you appreciate about yourself that have nothing to do with your appearance. Here are some questions to get you started:

* What's been your passion, ever since you were little?
* What relationships are meaningful to you?
* How do you treat others?
* What is your hidden talent?
* What are you most proud of?

Now type out what you "weigh," and place the words over a photo of yourself. You can share this I Weigh post with others or keep it to yourself. Either way, continue adding to your list whenever you think of something else you love about yourself. If you're ever feeling insignificant or in need of a little loving, read over the list to remember how incredible you are.

#iweigh @i_weigh:

my competitiveness in card games

willingness to try new things

hair-washing boycotts

work ethic

laughs with my brother

love of mac n cheese

incredible ability to spill literally everything

Exercising Love

What is your biggest motivation for exercising?

I talked with Maris Degener, a yoga teacher, anorexia survivor, and the subject of the documentary *I Am Maris*. She believes a lot of us go into a workout with the goal of diminishing ourselves. We think, *I can burn calories, I can lose weight, I can make myself physically smaller.* When we approach exercise in this way, it feels like punishment.

But there is a different way to exercise, which is a form of self-love. Maris calls it the "abundance mindset." This means that we work out in order to feel good, both physically and mentally. Maris suggests that we go into a workout thinking, *What can this movement bring to me? What can it add to my experience and my well-being?* Maybe exercise clears our mind, makes us feel calm, or challenges us to listen to our body.

You might be thinking, *Don't we* need *to push ourselves hard to get better at anything?* Sure. There's nothing wrong with challenging ourselves, as long as our main goal in exercising is a loving one.

The next time you are exercising, take a moment to check in with your motives. Why are you doing this? Is it punishment for being "lazy" over the weekend? Try shifting that to a positive: relieving your stress, or strengthening your muscles.

Q&A

Q: I get the concept of being kind to ourselves when we exercise. But what do I do if I'm in a fitness class and the instructor is being . . . uh . . . less than loving?

A: If we're in a group setting, like gym class or yoga, it can be extra hard to keep in the abundance mindset, because we feel pressure to do everything our instructor tells us. However, we can still exercise with self-love. Sometimes that means leaving the class.

I was in a yoga class with a new teacher who was really negative and pushy. He started chastising me and repositioning my body into uncomfortable positions. I told him "That hurts" and "Please stop," yet he continued repositioning my body. Finally I just got up and walked out of the studio. It was extremely awkward in front of the whole class, but it didn't feel right to continue. I knew I had to leave.

Some situations might not be physically dangerous but still make you feel bad about yourself or push you to override your body's instincts. If that's the case, it's always okay to talk with the instructor and explain how you feel. You might decide to modify some of the exercises to help you feel better. Maris also points out that if we're struggling to exercise in the abundance mindset, a group setting might not be the best option. Maybe we can better practice self-love by exercising with a video at home.

HEART OPENER

This simple yoga pose opens up the area surrounding the heart. When we stretch, it helps release any tension or stress we've been holding. That way we can be available to give love to ourselves and others.

1. Sit cross-legged on a comfortable surface. Breathe in, then out.

2. On an inhale, arch your back beginning at your tailbone, all the way up to your chest. Open your shoulders to shine your heart forward. Lift your gaze slightly upward. Press the tip of your tongue to the roof of your mouth, to protect your neck.

3. As you exhale, curl your spine back in, beginning at your tailbone and ending at your head. Separate your shoulder blades as your chest curves inward. Let your chin drop toward your chest.

4. Repeat this cycle in line with your breath for as long as you'd like. Then switch the crossing of your legs and repeat on the other side.

Lavender Rose Chocolate Truffles

These truffles taste like pure love in food form. Their delicate flavors of lavender and rose are bound to make you feel special. They're silky, smooth, and rich—a chocolate lover's dream.

YIELD: 16 TRUFFLES  *option*

Ingredients

½ cup coconut cream, from the top of a chilled 13½-ounce can of full-fat coconut milk

1½ cups dark chocolate chips or chopped dark chocolate*

2 drops food-grade pure lavender oil

¼ cup cacao powder

2 Tbsp dried rose petals, crushed

 To make this recipe sugar-free, use stevia-sweetened dark chocolate.

Instructions

1. Scoop the coconut cream into a double boiler (instructions on page 11). Heat the coconut cream until it's hot to the touch, then pour in the chocolate. Turn the heat down to medium-low. Stir the chocolate and coconut cream together until the chocolate is fully melted and the mixture forms a shiny ganache.

2. Remove the ganache from heat and stir in the lavender oil. Place the bowl of ganache in the refrigerator to chill for 2 hours, or until completely solid.

3. Line a plate with parchment paper. Scoop the chocolate mixture into 16 pieces using a tablespoon, and place on the plate. Don't worry about forming the pieces into spheres yet. Place the plate back in the refrigerator for 10 minutes to firm up.

4. Pour the cacao powder and crushed rose petals into 2 small separate bowls. Roll the refrigerated chocolate blobs into balls, then roll them in either cacao powder, rose petals, or leave them plain. Serve.

5. Store leftovers in an airtight container in the refrigerator for about 1 week, or freeze for up to 1 month. Defrost before serving.

Mexican Wedding Cookies

These cookies are buttery, crispy, and full of pecans. They have been a part of Mexican wedding festivities for a long time, so they're a perfect symbol of love. I like to make them for family and friends around the holiday season, but they're yummy any time of year.

YIELD: 12 COOKIES    *option*

Ingredients

1¾ cups blanched almond flour

¼ cup arrowroot flour

¼ tsp sea salt

6 Tbsp sustainable palm shortening

3 Tbsp pure maple syrup*

½ cup toasted pecans, chopped into small pieces

½ cup organic powdered sugar**

Instructions

1. Preheat your oven to 350°F and line a cookie sheet with parchment paper.

2. In a large bowl, whisk together the almond flour, arrowroot flour, and sea salt. Add the palm shortening, maple syrup, and toasted pecans. Stir using a rubber spatula until the mixture forms a dough.

3. Scoop the dough into 12 balls using a 1½-tablespoon cookie scoop, and place them at least 1 inch apart on the prepared cookie sheet. Bake the cookies for 12 to 14 minutes, or until they are golden brown on top. Let the cookies cool for 10 minutes on the cookie sheet.

4. Sift the powdered sugar into a small bowl to remove any lumps. Roll the cookies in the sugar one by one, coating all sides. When ready to serve, sift a bit more powdered sugar onto the cookies. These cookies are best eaten the day they're made. Leftovers can be stored at room temperature on a plate lightly covered with tin foil for a up to 4 days, but they will lose their crunch over time.

 To make this recipe sugar-free, replace the pure maple syrup with monk fruit maple-flavored syrup and use powdered monk fruit sweetener (see below).

**Powdered cane sugar (made with tapioca starch) is the whitest in color, but it's not Paleo. For a Paleo option, use powdered maple sugar, which you can make by blending 1 cup maple sugar in your blender until powdery. For a sugar-free option, blend classic monk fruit sweetener into powder using your blender.*

Raspberry Mini Bundt Cakes

These cakes are light and moist, with fresh raspberries and mild honey icing. Show someone in your life a little love and give them one of these delightful mini bundts.

YIELD: 9 MINI BUNDT CAKES

Ingredients

CAKE

¾ cup fresh raspberries, chopped in half, if large

¾ cup + 1 Tbsp arrowroot flour, divided, plus more for dusting

1¾ cups blanched almond flour

3 Tbsp coconut flour

1 tsp baking soda

¼ tsp sea salt

5 large eggs

¾ cup pure maple syrup or honey

¼ cup coconut oil or sustainable palm shortening, melted, plus more for greasing

3 Tbsp full-fat coconut milk (from one of the cans used in the icing)

⅓ cup fresh lemon juice

ICING

1 cup coconut cream, from the tops of 2 chilled 13½-ounce cans of full-fat coconut milk

2 Tbsp honey

Instructions

1. Preheat your oven to 350°F. Grease a mini bundt pan (or muffin tin) with some coconut oil, and sprinkle lightly with arrowroot flour. In a small bowl, toss together the raspberries and 1 Tbsp arrowroot flour. Set aside.

2. In a large bowl, whisk together the almond flour, remaining ¾ cup arrowroot flour, coconut flour, baking soda, and sea salt. In a separate large bowl, whisk together the eggs, maple syrup, coconut oil, coconut milk, and lemon juice. Stir the wet ingredients into the dry and mix using a rubber spatula just until combined.

3. Let the batter sit for 10 minutes, to thicken. Gently fold in the arrowroot flour–coated raspberries. Pour ½ cup batter into each well of the mini bundt pan (since mine has 6 wells, I did 2 batches). Bake for 18 to 23 minutes, or until the bundts are golden brown and spring back when touched.

4. Let the bundts cool for 25 minutes. Carefully run a toothpick around the outside and center hole of each, then release the cakes onto a cooling rack. Regrease and flour the bundt pan, then bake the remaining batter.

5. Make the icing by combining the coconut cream and honey in a small saucepan over medium heat and bringing to a simmer. Let it simmer for 5 to 10 minutes, or until it becomes syrupy and thick. Remove from heat.

6. Drizzle the icing over the bundt cakes and serve. Store bundts and icing separately in airtight containers in the refrigerator for up to 1 week.

CHAPTER TWO
Be Bossy

The B-Word

In second grade, I was working on a class project about the Amazon rain forest. I was excited because my group got to make a giant poster covered in trees, parrots, and jaguars. I was in the flow, sharing my ideas with the other kids on how we could make our poster even better.

All of a sudden, one of the boys said, "Sadie, stop being so bossy."

I closed my mouth. This was the first time someone had called me that. I was embarrassed and confused. Was I being too assertive by being a leader of the project? Or by giving suggestions? I was proud of my knack for organizing groups and coming up with ideas. I didn't think there was anything wrong with that. In fact, I thought people appreciated it. But now I was being insulted for that very habit. I stayed quiet for the rest of class.

Over the years, classmates continued to call me bossy: a boy in fifth-grade history class, a girl in eighth-grade gym class, a boy in tenth-grade math class. Eventually I realized that they kept calling me bossy because I *am* bossy. It's been in my nature since I was a baby. But it's not something to be ashamed of—it can be a strength. It's what makes me strong-willed, productive, and, okay . . . maybe . . . *sometimes* . . . a little feared.

Hear Her

I wanted to hear other young women's experiences with being called bossy, so I texted a bunch of them and asked. Here's what they said:

I have always been called bossy. It dulls my light a bit each time.

I wonder if I'm taking up too much space when I take charge, or if someone else is better qualified to lead.

I tend to be quieter in conversations, so I've never been called bossy. But I have heard things like, "Oh, you're a <u>smart girl</u>."

It hurts my feelings when I'm called bossy so I just try to shut those memories out.

As a young girl, being called things like that didn't really bother me, so I shook it off. But I think they've subconsciously stuck with me and made me more hesitant to take charge.

I feel like "You're so bossy" could be a rite of passage to womanhood at this point.

Tomato/Tomahto

Have you ever heard a man or boy called "bossy"? Probably not. When males are forceful, they're praised for their take-charge attitude. This is because they're raised to be leaders. Meanwhile, females are taught that men should be in charge and that we should take the passenger seat. Words such as *bossy* are used for females when someone feels threatened by our confidence, intellect, or leadership and wants to put us in our place.

The Economist observed this double standard by looking at phrases commonly used to describe men and women. They found that certain words are used almost exclusively to put down women, while nearly the exact same traits are used to *praise* men. Here are some examples:

MEN		WOMEN
Assertive	»	Pushy
Persistent	»	Nagging
Frustrated	»	Upset
Has a lot to say	»	Chatty

So what can we do about this double standard?

Let's start by treating words such as *bossy* as a compliment. Bossy can be powerful. Instead of shying away from it, let's be bossier than ever. From working on group projects in second grade to speaking on the House floor in Washington, DC, let's be as expressive and bold as boys are taught to be—more, even.

Of course, part of being bossy is being respectful and kind. While we're being assertive, we can honor other people's voices at the same time.

Here are some ways you can flex your bossiness:

- Raise your hand in class more often.
- Speak up when you disagree with somebody's opinion.
- Place yourself in charge of a project or group.
- When someone talks over you, finish your thought instead of automatically yielding.

This last one might feel super awkward. But it can also be a winning strategy. Kieran Snyder, a tech entrepreneur, found that during meetings, men interrupted the person speaking twice as often as women did. But she noticed something surprising: there were three women who interrupted as often as men did; each woman was a top-tier executive at the company. So, in order to advance our careers, it may help to learn how to interrupt and talk over people—an art men have so wonderfully mastered!

Be the Boss

Across the globe, women and girls are expressing their strong personalities more than ever. They're becoming entrepreneurs and CEOs, and surprising the world with their bossiness. Mikaila Ulmer is one of them. At age four, Mikaila started a company called Me & the Bees Lemonade. Now she's in high school and her company is booming. Between school and sports Mikaila still finds time to present at trade shows, speak to thousands of people, and take meetings with investors—flexing her bossy muscle all the while. Oh, and she once introduced President Barack Obama at a national summit!

Mikaila told me that adults have underestimated her since she was a little girl. "I'm an African American, I'm fourteen years old, I'm a female," she said. Many people automatically assume she's too young to have a successful business. One investor asked Mikaila if she squeezes the lemons herself. She calmly replied, "No, I have an actual lemonade company; it's in eighteen hundred stores."

But along with being underestimated can come immense satisfaction. Throughout her meetings and speeches, Mikaila is helping to fight against the double standard. She says it's "pretty gratifying when you're able to break stereotypes of who can be a successful entrepreneur and inspire others to do the same."

Q&A

Q: I'm trying to get more comfortable sharing my opinions in class. But some kids still roll their eyes and mumble that I'm being bossy or pushy. What can I say to them?

A: Use it as a teaching moment! Respond in a way that helps other people recognize the double standard. You could try one of these:

- "Thank you!" (my personal favorite)
- "I must have misunderstood—I thought we could voice our opinions."
- "If you have another idea, I'm all ears."

MINDFUL MOVEMENT
WARRIOR II

This yoga pose helps us feel as strong as warriors. When our legs root firmly into the ground and our arms shoot outward, we get in touch with the power and energy inside us. This pose is great when you want to hone your bossy skills.

1. You can do this pose on any flat, even surface. Begin by standing with your feet apart and parallel, wider than your hips, but not so wide that you feel unbalanced.

2. Turn your right leg out to the right, toes perpendicular to your left foot. Now turn your left leg slightly in, to the right.

3. Press your feet into the floor. Lift your arms up and out to your sides, parallel to the ground. Take a deep breath in.

4. On the exhale, bend your right knee so your leg is close to a 90-degree angle. Make sure you can see your right big toe on the inside of your knee.

5. Take a few deep breaths with your leg bent. Look past your right middle fingertip and imagine it shooting out lightning. Feel your strength and power.

6. On an inhale, straighten your right leg and lift your waist up, then exhale and bend your right knee, rooting deeper toward the ground. Continue this pattern for a few breaths: inhale, straighten, and get taller through the top of your head; exhale and bend your right leg.

7. Lower your arms and turn your toes back in. Repeat this process on your left side.

Avocado Chocolate Mousse

This chocolate mousse is velvety, thick, and rich with dark chocolate. Thanks to avocado, it's also full of brain-boosting healthy fats that help us function in boss mode.

YIELD: SERVES 4–5    *option*

Ingredients

4 ripe avocados, pitted and peeled

¾ cup cacao powder

½ cup + 2 Tbsp maple syrup *

1 Tbsp water

2 tsp vanilla extract

2 Tbsp cacao nibs, for garnish (optional)

 To make this recipe sugar-free, replace the pure maple syrup with monk fruit maple-flavored syrup.

Instructions

1. Combine the avocado, cacao powder, maple syrup, water, and vanilla extract in a high-speed blender. Blend until smooth, using your blender's tamper, if you have one. You may need to add another tablespoon of water to help it blend.

2. Scoop the mousse into an airtight container and place in the refrigerator to chill for 1 hour, or serve immediately. Scoop the mousse into individual bowls, garnish with nibs, if using, and serve right away. Store leftovers in an airtight container in the refrigerator for up to 3 days.

Matcha Dream Bars

These bars are bold. They have a ridiculously good flavor from tahini (ground sesame seeds) and matcha (a green tea from Japan). This combination creates the most satisfying dessert: a crunchy, salty tahini-cashew crust, a super-creamy matcha filling, and a silky smooth chocolate ganache. While you eat them, daydream about what type of boss you plan to be!

YIELD: 16 BARS    *option*

Ingredients

CRUST

1 cup unsweetened shredded coconut

¾ cup roasted unsalted cashews

⅓ cup tahini

2 Tbsp pure maple syrup*

¼ tsp sea salt

MATCHA CREAM FILLING

2 cups roasted unsalted cashews

⅔ cup coconut cream, from the top of a chilled 13½-ounce can of full-fat coconut milk

2 Tbsp liquid from the bottom of the coconut milk can

2 Tbsp coconut oil

2 Tbsp pure maple syrup*

1½ tsp matcha green tea powder

CHOCOLATE GANACHE

2 Tbsp coconut cream, from the top of a chilled 13½-ounce can of full-fat coconut milk

½ cup chopped dark chocolate*

2 Tbsp coconut oil

Instructions

1. Line the bottom and sides of an 8 x 8-inch baking dish with parchment paper.

2. In a high-speed blender, blend together all the crust ingredients until the ingredients get broken down into tiny pieces and a thick dough forms. Periodically scrape down the sides of the blender with a rubber spatula in between blending. Don't overblend!

3. Press the crust evenly into the prepared baking dish and place it in the freezer for 10 minutes.

4. Place all the filling ingredients in the blender and blend until smooth and creamy. It may help to use your blender's tamper, if you have one. Pour the filling into the crust and freeze for 30 minutes, or until solid.

5. Combine all ganache ingredients and melt together in a double boiler over medium-high heat (instructions on page 11). Or melt by pouring the ingredients into a heatproof bowl and microwaving in 30-second intervals, stirring the chocolate each time.

6. Pour the ganache on top of the matcha filling, spreading it out evenly. Freeze for approximately 30 minutes, or until firm. Slice into 16 squares and serve. Store leftover bars in an airtight container in the freezer for up to 1 month. Defrost for a few minutes before eating.

 To make this recipe sugar-free, replace the maple syrup with monk fruit maple-flavored syrup and use stevia-sweetened dark chocolate

Mexican Hot Chocolate

This hot chocolate is a little bit sweet, a little bit fiery—just like you! It gets its kick from cinnamon and a hint of cayenne pepper, which give it a complex flavor. The best part is you can adjust the spiciness and sweetness to your liking. Not a spicy person? Omit the cayenne. Don't like things too sweet? Use less monk fruit extract. You're the boss of this recipe—and this life!

YIELD: SERVES 2

Ingredients

One 13½-ounce can of full-fat coconut milk

¾ cup water

¼ cup cacao powder

1 tsp vanilla extract

1 tsp ground cinnamon

A few shakes cayenne pepper, to taste

¼ tsp liquid monk fruit extract or stevia extract, to taste

3 Tbsp coconut cream, from the top of a chilled 13½-ounce can of full-fat coconut milk, for topping (optional)

Instructions

1. Combine the coconut milk and water in a saucepan over medium-high heat and bring to a simmer.

2. Remove from heat, then pour into a high-speed blender. Add the cacao powder, vanilla extract, cinnamon, and cayenne pepper. Blend (carefully, as the mixture is hot) until the drink is smooth and creamy. Slowly add in the monk fruit extract little by little, adjusting to your liking.

3. If topping with coconut cream, scoop the coconut cream into a small bowl. Whisk vigorously using a fork, just until smooth. Pour the hot chocolate into 2 mugs, top with the whipped coconut cream, if using, and serve.

CHAPTER THREE

Be Light

Choose Your Light

What's the first thing that comes to your mind when you think about being "light"? It's one of those words with a bunch of meanings.

light.

adj. Having little weight; not heavy.

The word *light* often makes people think of the weight-related definition. It brings to mind numbers on a scale, weight loss, or diet products. It often evokes stress and heavy feelings.

That's not the kind of lightness I'm talking about. *Light* has other positive, powerful, and useful definitions for us. Reclaiming this one word can help shift our entire perspective.

light.

adj. Having less baggage or load; requiring little effort.

adj. Gentle.

Sometimes when we eat, we carry the weight of society's judgments on our shoulders. The other day I had pizza for dinner. As I put a slice up to my mouth, I heard the voice of someone on Instagram last week saying that we should avoid pizza at all cost. So as I took a bite, I thought, *I shouldn't be eating this . . .*

Sometimes we even feel guilty just for *thinking* about food. The subject weighs us down. If we can lighten the charge of food, we will be gentler to ourselves.

n. Illumination.

n. Something that informs or clarifies.

Shedding light on something illuminates it, helping us see it in a whole new way. What if we shed some of that light on our food? Our culture has made food so confusing and scary, it has become like an enemy. This is *insane.* Food is a wonderful, necessary part of everyone's life. It should be a powerful ally, not a burden.

A New Friend

To shed a new light on food and make friends with it, we first need to get to know it better—like that intriguing girl in school who you never got to know but always wanted to. There are so many fun experiences just waiting to happen between you two. Here's how to start that friendship.

1. SOURCE IT

Many foods are processed and packaged until it's hard to know what we're even eating. We need to get back to the source and see where our food comes from. Here are some of my favorite ways:

* **Visit a local farmer's market.** As you walk past the stalls, get lost in the abundance of fresh, colorful fruits and veggies. Stop and talk to farmers and learn about their favorite ingredients in season. Pick up some items that look beautiful and exciting.

* **Take a trip to an ethnic grocery store.** Pick out five foods you have never heard of. I recently went shopping at a Vietnamese market, where I was introduced to a world of new ingredients and flavors. I was inspired to go home and make pho.

* **Stop by a supermarket.** Even a large chain store can have really interesting ingredients! The key is to skip the center aisles (where all the processed foods are) and scour the outskirts. Talk with an employee in the produce section to learn what's in season. Try to pick out five fruits, vegetables, or meats that look delicious and that you have never eaten before.

2. STUDY IT

It's exciting to arrive home with a bag full of new foods. But after unloading the groceries, you might feel a bit lost. *What in the world am I going to do with this giant spaghetti squash?* This is where the internet comes into play. Enter the name of one of your ingredients and "recipe" into a search engine to learn more about the food's origins, flavors, and the best ways to prepare it. When we research new foods and learn all about them, they become less scary and more exciting. So shine that light brightly!

3. SIZZLE IT

Once you've found a yummy-looking recipe, roll up your sleeves and get cooking. You can make just one entrée or dessert, or try taking on a full meal. You're embarking on a creative adventure. Feel free to toss in whatever spices or herbs smell good. Taste your dish as you go, noticing every nuance of the food. Part of befriending food is having fun with it. Don't be afraid to go wild and make a mess of your kitchen!

Working with new ingredients is an intimate experience. It will help you grow closer to food than ever before.

4. SAVOR IT

As you sit down to eat, appreciate the fact that you gathered the ingredients yourself and transformed them into a delicious dish or meal. If you eat with loved ones, you can also feel the satisfaction of sharing it with them. If the food isn't super delicious on your first try, don't worry. Mine sure isn't always! But we all improve with practice.

When you dig in, savor each bite. How does it taste? What aromas can you smell? What texture does the food have as you chew? Notice each aspect of your meal and how it makes you feel. Eating in this way—slowly and with gratitude—is one of the best things you can do to lighten and brighten your relationship with food.

You can take this new appreciation of food into each day of your life. If you're scarfing down eggs for breakfast or demolishing a sandwich at lunch, slow down. Savor it. Feel a moment of gratitude for all the plants, animals, and people who helped create this meal for you.

Q&A

Q: I'm super busy and just don't have the time to cook. How can I still have a closer connection with food?

A: Luckily it's still possible to enjoy good food even when you rarely have time to cook or to eat at home. One great trick is to make your own lunches ahead of time. All it takes is a little planning and preparation and your delicious, wholesome lunch will be ready when you run out the door.

> **Plan.** On Saturday, decide what things you want to have for lunch next week. I like to plan two main courses along with a few snacks, to last the whole week (ideas below). Then go shopping for all the ingredients you'll need.

> **Prep.** On Sunday, prepare all the ingredients for the week's meals. This usually entails some chopping, sautéing, maybe some baking. But this prep won't take very long. Just store everything in the fridge so it's ready to go.

> **Pack.** Each morning, assemble your main course and pop it into your bag. Throw in a couple of snacks, and you're all set!

Turkey Sandwich with Fluffy Sandwich Bread
- Ingredients: Fluffy Sandwich Bread (page 52), humanely raised turkey or chicken lunch meat, lettuce, tomato, Paleo mayo
- Prep: Make the bread, slice tomato, and place in a small container.

Collard Greens Wrap
- Ingredients: collard greens, sweet potatoes, red bell peppers, carrots, humanely raised turkey or chicken lunch meat, Paleo mayo
- Prep: De-stem the collard greens and blanch them by placing them in boiling water for 1 minute, then let them cool. Store in a bag in the fridge. Chop the veggies and roast for 25 minutes, then store in a container in the fridge.

Tuna Salad
- Ingredients: wild-caught canned tuna, Paleo mayo, celery
- Prep: Chop the celery, stir together the tuna and mayo, and throw in the celery.

Chopped Salad
- Ingredients: romaine lettuce, eggs, pumpkin seeds, tomatoes, balsamic vinegar, olive oil
- Prep: Chop the lettuce and place in a bowl. Make 12 hard-boiled eggs and slice, then place in a separate small bowl. You can use however many you want for your salad and save the rest for later this week! Slice tomatoes and place in another bowl. Combine the vinegar and oil in a small dish.

MINDFUL MOVEMENT
HALF SUN SALUTATION

When I flow through this yoga sequence first thing in the morning, it fills me with energy for the day. It also creates an awesome stretch in my back and legs. You can do this pose at any time of day, whenever you want a boost of energy.

1. Find a flat, even surface. Stand with your feet hip width apart. Bring your palms together at your heart and take a few deep breaths.

2. On an inhale, reach your arms out wide and lift them above your head. As you exhale, bend forward and sweep your arms down to the ground.

3. Fold your body over your legs and bring your belly close to your thighs. Make sure to bend your knees if you can't get close to your legs with them straight, to protect your lower back. Take a few breaths here.

4. Bend your knees more. On an inhale, open your chest as you shine your heart forward.

5. Exhale as you fold over your legs again. Take a few deep breaths.

6. On an inhale, stand up and sweep your arms over your head. Exhale and bring your hands to your heart.

7. Stand with your hands at your heart, breathing, and have a moment of stillness, just noticing the feeling of your body on the earth. Repeat this sequence a few more times, moving through the postures fluidly and with your breath, until you feel filled with energy.

Cookie Dough Truffles

When you're craving dessert but don't want to go through all the work of baking, these cookie dough truffles are here for you. They require a very light amount of effort, with an incredibly yummy, seriously addictive result. Prep these at the beginning of the week so each day after school or work you can arrive home to a fridge full of cookie dough balls!

YIELD: 10–12 TRUFFLES  *option*

Ingredients

1½ cups blanched almond flour

2 Tbsp arrowroot flour

2 Tbsp ground golden flaxseed

¼ tsp sea salt

¼ cup sustainable palm shortening, melted*

¼ cup pure maple syrup**

1 tsp vanilla extract

¼ cup dark chocolate chips or chopped dark chocolate**

COATING (OPTIONAL)

1 cup dark chocolate chips or chopped dark chocolate**

1 tsp flaky sea salt (optional)

Instructions

1. In a medium bowl, whisk together the almond flour, arrowroot flour, ground golden flaxseed, and sea salt.

2. Add in the palm shortening, maple syrup, and vanilla extract, and stir just until combined. Fold in ¼ cup chocolate chips.

3. Line a plate with parchment paper. Using a 1½-tablespoon cookie scoop or heaping tablespoon, scoop the cookie dough into 10 to 12 balls and place on the plate. Freeze the cookie dough balls for 30 minutes, or until firm. Serve right away or continue to make the coating.

4. To make the coating, melt the chocolate chips in a double boiler over medium-high heat (instructions on page 11). Or melt by pouring the chocolate into a heatproof bowl and microwaving in 30-second intervals, stirring the chocolate each time.

5. Using a fork, dunk all of the cookie dough balls in the melted chocolate (or half of them, as pictured). Once each ball is completely coated, place it back on the plate and sprinkle with flaky sea salt, if using.

6. Freeze the balls for 30 minutes, then serve. Store leftovers in an airtight container in the refrigerator for up to 1 week, or in the freezer for up to 3 months.

 If you tolerate dairy, I highly recommend using grass-fed butter in place of the shortening here for an incredible flavor!

** To make this recipe sugar-free, replace the pure maple syrup with monk fruit maple-flavored syrup and use stevia-sweetened dark chocolate chips.*

Fluffy Sandwich Bread

Have you run yourself ragged trying to make different lunches every day? Try this miracle recipe. Making a loaf of this bread will lighten your workload because you can eat it all week for avocado toast, French toast, sandwiches—you name it! You only need five ingredients and a blender. No yeast or flour!

YIELD: 1 LOAF; 12 TO 14 SLICES (SF)

Ingredients

2 cups roasted cashews
or cashew pieces
(unsalted or salted)

6 large eggs

¼ cup full-fat coconut milk

2 Tbsp ground golden flaxseed

1 Tbsp apple cider vinegar

1 tsp baking soda

¼ tsp sea salt

Instructions

1. Preheat your oven to 350°F and line the sides and bottom of an 8½ x 4½-inch glass loaf pan with parchment paper.

2. Using a high-speed blender, blend together all ingredients until smooth and free of lumps. It may help to use your blender's tamper, if you have one.

3. Pour the batter into the lined loaf pan and bake for 35 to 38 minutes, or until the loaf is golden brown and a toothpick inserted into the center comes out clean. Let the loaf cool for 15 minutes, then slice into 12 to 14 slices.

4. Store the bread in an airtight container at room temperature for up to 4 days, no toasting necessary. For longer storage, store in the freezer for up to 1 month. Reheat in the toaster.

Strawberry Coconut Macaroons

These cookies are as light as clouds, with a soft interior and crispy edges. The addition of freeze-dried strawberries adds a bright pop of flavor.

YIELD: 16–18 MACAROONS

Ingredients

5 large eggs

2 cups finely shredded unsweetened coconut

1½ cups freeze-dried strawberries, roughly chopped

¼ cup pure maple sugar*

¼ cup honey or pure maple syrup

 *If you don't have maple sugar on hand, you can substitute coconut sugar, but just know it will give the macaroons a slightly darker color.

Instructions

1. Preheat your oven to 350°F and line a cookie sheet with parchment paper.

2. Separate the egg yolks from the egg whites (you can find helpful video tutorials for this on the internet). We're only using the egg whites for this recipe, so you can either discard the egg yolks or save them for another day.

3. Place the egg whites in the bowl of a stand mixer, or use a large bowl and a handheld mixer. Whip on high until the egg whites become super fluffy and they form medium peaks when you flip the whisk upside down.

4. Using a rubber spatula, gently fold in the coconut, freeze-dried strawberries, maple sugar, and honey.

5. Using a 1½-tablespoon cookie scoop or a heaping tablespoon, pack the dough into balls and place on the cookie sheet.

6. Bake the macaroons for 22 to 25 minutes, or until golden brown. Let them cool fully before serving. These cookies are best eaten the day they're made, but leftovers may be stored in an airtight container at room temperature for up to 5 days.

CHAPTER FOUR

Be Deep

The Here and Now

What if you could change your life by doing one thing for just ten seconds each day? What if this thing would make you more contented, more grounded, and less stressed?

Welcome to mindfulness.

We spend almost all of our time worrying about two things: what has already happened (the past) and what hasn't happened yet (the future). This only makes us miserable. The past is over, so there's nothing we can do about it. And the future isn't something we should be thinking about right now—unless we're taking concrete action toward a goal.

Mindfulness breaks us out of this pattern by turning our awareness to the simple moments of life *as they happen.* We laser in on our senses as we're experiencing them, and we feel them deeply.

So, the way to "be deep" is to focus on what's going on *right now.*

I first learned about mindfulness in yoga class. At the end of the class, the teacher had everyone lie down and enter *savasana,* or final relaxation. We practiced tuning in to our senses and letting go of our thoughts. It was exactly as hard as it sounds!

Sometimes a *savasana* would go by where I literally never stopped thinking. But as I practiced, I got a little better at letting go of thoughts as they came. I learned how to take just one breath without my mind going wild. I began experimenting with taking that mindfulness with me, off the yoga mat and into the rest of my life. I practiced coming into the present moment at different points throughout the day. Every time, I felt deeply connected with myself and the world around me. It was liberating.

I have two favorite ways to zap into the present moment.

The first way is to briefly tune in to my breath a few times a day. Set an alarm on your watch or phone to go off at three set times during the day. When it goes off, close your eyes and take three deep breaths. Notice how the breath feels as it flows in and out. Let go of whatever else is going on in your mind. Then open your eyes and go back to your day.

The second way is to tune in to the little details of the day. Say you're picking up a water bottle. Consider this: How does the bottle feel in your hand? Is it heavy or light? When you take a sip of the water, how does it feel on your tongue? Is it cool or warm? What does it taste like? Try this exercise with one small act each day.

These short exercises are my favorite ways to be deep. Once you've done these exercises, try a full mindfulness meditation to dive even deeper into the moment (see Seated Meditation, page 148).

Shallow Waters

We are never less deep than when we're on social media.

The other day, on Instagram, I posted a photo of myself with my dog. I was holding him in my arms, and he looked exactly like a teddy bear—definite "like" bait. Later that day I checked the post. It had way less likes than I expected. I actually felt a pit in my stomach. I felt way worse than before I turned on my phone. (Every time I open up social media, I end up feeling bad about something. It might be losing followers, not getting comments, or wishing I had more direct messages.)

I got to thinking about how I interact with other people's posts. A lot of the time, when I "like" a photo, I put very little thought into it. It's a mindless, zoned-out process of tapping and scrolling. I usually don't even read the captions. I just double tap, scroll, double tap, scroll, comment, scroll—endlessly. Really deep and thoughtful, right?

If I don't put much care into my social media interactions, then other people probably don't, either. That means that the number of likes and comments I get has little, if anything, to do with me! *Almost none of it is personal.*

But the illusion is strong. It feels as if likes actually represent how many people like us in real life. I can't tell you how many times I've decided that a friend wasn't into me anymore just because they didn't comment on my latest post. But usually when I see that friend in person, I realize that everything is totally fine. This is crazy! We have no idea what a friend might be going through privately, why they're not on social media, or why they didn't "like"—or even see—our post.

These online connections are *not* real-life relationships. So the more we can detach from the results of our online interactions, the better. But it's hard! I still get a flutter of excitement when someone leaves a nice comment on a post. And I feel dejected when I lose followers.

The next time something on social media makes you feel at all crummy, try this: close your eyes, turn off your phone, and take a very deep breath.

Q&A

Q: It seems like my friends and I only communicate through social media. How can I connect with them in a deeper way?

A: The best way to connect with someone is by having an actual real-life conversation. In person is the best, but talking on the phone is good, too. The other day I saw a post by a friend whom I hadn't seen in a while. I missed her, so I decided to call her on the phone. She picked up! I asked how she was doing. She said her family was going through a rough time and we talked about that for a while. She was grateful that I had called.

Our relationship was instantly strengthened through a quick conversation. Talking with a person, even briefly, takes more effort than commenting on their Instagram posts. It can also feel awkward to call. Maybe they're in the middle of something and don't want to talk. Or maybe they won't answer, and we'll have to leave an annoying voicemail. Maybe we'll seem needy! But when we make the effort to talk with someone, it gives us a deep connection that social media never can. It makes us feel valued, and the other person will appreciate the effort we took. It's worth it, I promise.

MINDFUL MOVEMENT
WALKING MEDITATION

Walking meditation is a great way to de-stress and get centered while moving your body and getting some fresh air. It takes only a few minutes, so you can do it almost anywhere.

1. The next time you're walking down the street, start by getting your senses alert. Tune in to the pace of your steps and fall into the rhythm of the steps. What do they sound like?

2. Turn your attention to an object you see as you're walking. It might be a sign, a tree, or a building. Look intently at that object and observe it without labeling it. Just notice it.

3. Now turn your attention to the noises that surround you. Don't label them. Just listen.

4. Finally, turn your attention to your breathing. Is it fast and shallow or slow and deep? Take a few deep breaths and continue with your steady pace.

5. When you finish your walk, take a minute and pause before reentering your day. Notice the way your body and mind feel. Carry that alertness and presence with you into the rest of your day.

Iced Gingerbread Cake

My favorite form of mindfulness meditation is baking. You can probably guess why! While you make this spicy, moist gingerbread cake, work with intention and care to make it the yummiest meditation practice imaginable.

YIELD: 16 SQUARES

Ingredients

CAKE

4 large eggs

⅓ cup blackstrap molasses

¼ cup coconut oil, melted

1 tsp vanilla extract

1 cup blanched almond flour

¼ cup arrowroot flour

¼ cup golden monk fruit sweetener*

2 Tbsp coconut flour

1 tsp baking soda

1 Tbsp ground ginger

1½ tsp ground cinnamon

½ tsp ground cloves

¼ tsp sea salt

ICING

¾ cup + 2 Tbsp coconut cream, from the tops of 2 chilled 13½-ounce cans of full-fat coconut milk

¼ cup coconut butter

1 Tbsp classic monk fruit sweetener*

Instructions

CAKE

1. Preheat your oven to 350°F and line the sides and bottom of an 8 x 8-inch square baking pan with parchment paper.

2. In a small bowl, whisk together the eggs, molasses, coconut oil, and vanilla extract until combined. In a medium bowl, whisk together the dry ingredients. Pour the wet ingredients into the dry and stir with a rubber spatula to remove any lumps in the batter.

3. Let the batter sit for 10 minutes, to thicken, then pour the batter into the prepared baking pan. Bake for approximately 30 minutes, or until a toothpick inserted in the center of the cake comes out clean. Let it cool to room temperature before icing.

ICING

1. Combine all the icing ingredients (except 2 Tbsp coconut cream) in a small saucepan over medium heat. Stir constantly.

2. Once the mixture is melted, bring it to a simmer and let it simmer for about 4 minutes, or until it has thickened considerably. Remove from heat and stir in the last 2 Tbsp coconut cream.

3. Let the icing cool for 5 minutes, then pour it over the cooled cake and spread evenly. Slice into 16 squares and serve. Store leftovers in an airtight container at room temperature for up to 3 days, or in the refrigerator for up to 1 week.

 If you're not worried about the recipe being low sugar, you can replace the monk fruit sweetener with maple sugar. Just know that the icing will be slightly less white.

Double Chocolate Vegan Brownies

These brownies are fudgy and gooey, with a flavor deep enough to satisfy even the hugest chocolate lover. I recently baked a batch for a birthday party, and many people came up to me after, asking how I made them. When I told them the ingredients, nobody could believe those brownies were vegan and Paleo!

YIELD: 9–12 BROWNIES  *option*

Ingredients

2 Tbsp ground golden flaxseed

6 Tbsp warm water

¾ cup creamy unsalted almond butter

6 Tbsp pure maple syrup*

⅓ cup cacao powder

¼ cup coconut sugar*

½ tsp baking soda

¼ tsp sea salt

⅓ cup chopped dark chocolate or dark chocolate chips*

Instructions

1. Preheat your oven to 350°F and line the bottom and sides of an 8 x 8-inch baking dish with parchment paper.

2. In a small bowl, whisk together the ground golden flaxseed and water to form a flax "egg." Set it aside for 5 minutes, or until it forms a gel.

3. In a medium bowl, whisk together the almond butter, maple syrup, and flax "egg." Add in the cacao powder, coconut sugar, baking soda, and sea salt. Stir just until combined using a rubber spatula. Fold in the chopped dark chocolate.

4. Pour the batter into the prepared baking dish. Bake brownies for 30 to 34 minutes, or until the middle is *just* solid to the touch. You want them to still be a little gooey on the inside.

5. Let the brownies cool for 15 minutes. Slice into 9 large brownies or 12 medium brownies and serve. Store leftovers in an airtight container at room temperature for up to 3 days, or in the refrigerator for up to 2 weeks.

 To make this recipe sugar-free, replace the pure maple syrup with monk fruit maple-flavored syrup, replace the coconut sugar with classic monk fruit sweetener, and use stevia-sweetened dark chocolate.

Zucchini Chocolate Chip Muffins

One of my favorite ways to connect with friends is by baking a special treat together. The process creates an occasion for us to share deep conversation and strengthen our bond. Invite a loved one over to hang out and cook these cinnamony chocolate-studded muffins!

YIELD: 10–12 MUFFINS   **SF** *option*

Ingredients

4 large eggs

⅓ cup pure maple syrup*

¼ cup coconut oil, melted

1 tsp vanilla extract

1 cup + 2 Tbsp blanched almond flour

¼ cup coconut flour

3 Tbsp arrowroot flour

1 tsp baking soda

1 tsp ground cinnamon

2 cups shredded zucchini (from about 2 medium zucchinis), with water squeezed out with paper towels after shredding

½ cup dark chocolate chips*

Instructions

1. Preheat your oven to 350°F and line a muffin tin with cupcake liners. (I like to use the natural nonstick variety.)

2. In a medium bowl, whisk together the eggs, maple syrup, coconut oil, and vanilla extract. In a large bowl, whisk together the almond flour, coconut flour, arrowroot flour, baking soda, and cinnamon. Whisk the wet ingredients into the dry and stir until smooth using a rubber spatula. Let the batter sit for 10 minutes, to thicken, then fold in the shredded zucchini and chocolate chips.

3. Scoop the batter evenly into the muffin tin. Bake the muffins for 25 to 28 minutes, or until a toothpick inserted into the center comes out clean. Let them cool for 10 minutes, then serve. Store leftover muffins in an airtight container at room temperature for up to 3 days, or refrigerate for up to 1 week.

 To make this recipe sugar-free, replace the pure maple syrup with monk fruit maple-flavored syrup and use stevia-sweetened chocolate chips.

CHAPTER FIVE

Be Unsure

I Don't Know

"What do you want to be when you grow up?"
"Where do you want to go to college?"
"What are you going to major in?"

When people ask these questions, I freak out. *Should I start thinking about a career? What college should I go to? Which major would best fit my future plans? What are my future plans? Why don't I have any future plans?*

And just like that, I enter a spiral of worry.

Mind reeling, wondering how to become a neurosurgeon (*Too many years in medical school?*), I finally manage to sputter out, "I don't know."

Because I *don't* know any of those things . . . at least not now. Maybe I'll know some of them next year, or maybe ten years from now. Maybe I'll never know for sure what I want to do when I grow up—even when I'm grown up. But right at this moment, I have no idea what my future will look like.

Some people know from a young age what they're going to be when they grow up. At three years old, Alyssa Carson knew she was going to be an astronaut. Now she's a young woman and training to be the first person to go to Mars. If you're like Alyssa and already know what you want to do, shout it from the rooftops!

But for most of us, we don't know what we want to do. And our plans change over time. So if you're feeling unsure about your future, don't let that scare you. Embrace the fact that you're exploring your options. It's actually super exciting.

By staying open, you have the chance to learn more about yourself and what energizes you. Maybe it's art or teaching or chemistry. Or maybe it's something that doesn't even exist yet. Right now, you can just try new things—join a new club, take a class that sounds interesting—and see if they light you up.

Also, when you're okay with being unsure, magical things can happen *because* you're not tied to one narrow version of yourself. Maybe a volunteer opportunity, internship, or job that you never dreamed of will suddenly appear.

Spiritual teacher Eckhart Tolle has a great explanation for this: "When you become comfortable with uncertainty, infinite possibilities open up in your life. It means fear is no longer a dominant factor in what you do and no longer prevents you from taking action to initiate change."

When we stop worrying about what the future will bring, we let go of fear.

So the next time someone asks you *any* question you don't know the answer to, respond with full confidence, "I don't know."

Now Is the New Know

Another benefit of uncertainty is that it helps us accept this moment—right now—and release our vision of what we think the future should look like. We don't need to know what our futures will look like. And we couldn't know anyway, even if we tried, because it's never the future yet; it's always *now*.

This is interesting to think about. Letting go of what we can't control allows us to live our lives in the present moment—which in turn allows us to take action. According to Tolle, that's because accepting this moment's uncertainty gives us "increased aliveness, alertness, and creativity."

Being comfortable with the unknown is a hard concept to put into practice. From an early age we're encouraged to always be thinking five steps ahead. *What will this lead to? How can this benefit me in the long run? Will this be on the final?*

To practice uncertainty, the next time you're doing any small activity—finishing an assignment, driving, doing the dishes—try focusing solely on that task without worrying about how it'll pan out in the end. Then, eventually, you will be able to take this concept of uncertainty out into bigger things in life, like applying for a job and then waiting for an offer.

Q&A

Q: I think my friends wonder who I like or what sexual orientation I am. Sometimes I wonder, too. What can I do to figure things out?

A: You're not alone in this uncertainty. I spoke with Stephanie Beatriz, an actress and bisexual activist. When she was a teenager, Stephanie was also confused about her sexuality. She thought, *I don't understand. I'm attracted to all genders . . . I'm not sure who that makes me.* To make matters worse, she saw nobody like her—a bisexual person—in the media or in her life. So she had nobody to look to for guidance. "I felt kind of lost," Stephanie says.

When we feel unsure, Stephanie encourages us to be aware of our feelings and to not rush to put ourselves in a category. "A label is only necessary if it means something to you," she says, "because you're the most important person in your own life." She also thinks labels can be dangerous because we label things so we can put them in a box, put them on a shelf, and not think about them anymore. As Stephanie says:

> *"Each of us is way more complex than just a label someone else has given us. If you're a young woman and you're listening to how other people label you, and believing that label, it doesn't give you room to grow outside of that box. You remain contained. But you're so much bigger than you could ever imagine."*

So if you're feeling outside pressure to label yourself, consider why that is. Who is putting that pressure on you? Is it your family, your friends, your social group at school? Or is it a greater feeling from society?

Even if all of your friends have labeled themselves, you don't have to do the same. You can say "I don't know." Responding in this way may make some friends or family members uncomfortable. That's okay.

If we do choose to label our sexuality or gender identity, Stephanie points out that we are ever-changing, so the label may not serve us forever. Your label "will change and fluctuate as you continue to create yourself in the world," she says. So don't get too attached to where you are right now, because things will ebb and flow with time. That's the beauty of being unsure!

MINDFUL MOVEMENT
CAT-COW POSE

In this rhythmic yoga sequence, we gently arch and round our back with the flow of our breath. It helps us get in touch with our body, so that we feel sure of ourselves no matter what lies ahead.

1. Find a flat, comfortable surface, such as a yoga mat, towel, or carpet.

2. Come onto your hands and knees. Make sure your hips are directly over your knees and your shoulders are over your wrists. Let your back be flat and neutral.

3. On an inhale, shine your heart forward. Slowly let your whole spine arch as your bottom ribs drop toward the floor. Release your shoulders away from your ears. You can slightly lift your gaze upward or keep your neck flat to relieve tension. Make sure the back of your neck stays long. This is "cow."

4. On the exhale, push your palms into the earth and curl your back in the opposite direction. Start by tucking your tailbone, then curling up your whole spine. Broaden your shoulder blades and breathe into the space there. Let your neck hang, relaxed. This is "cat."

5. Continue this pattern, moving slowly and deliberately: inhale, cow; exhale, cat. Repeat until you feel grounded in your body.

Salted Caramel Apples

Crisp apple slices dunked in creamy (but dairy-free) salted caramel sauce is the perfect fall dessert. Caramel sauce can be a little tricky to make because it's hard to know whether the caramel is overcooked or undercooked. So this recipe is great practice for letting go of control and jumping headfirst into uncertainty.

My favorite apples for this recipe are Honeycrisp and Granny Smith, because their tartness complements the sweet caramel. But any apples you have on hand will be just right!

YIELD: SERVES 10

Ingredients

½ cup coconut sugar

¾ cup full-fat coconut milk

2 tsp vanilla extract

1 tsp coconut oil

¼ tsp sea salt

5 apples, sliced

Instructions

1. Whisk together the coconut sugar and coconut milk in a medium saucepan and bring to a boil over medium-high heat.

2. Once the mixture has started boiling, turn down the heat to medium-low and let the caramel simmer for 20 to 25 minutes, whisking every couple minutes. If it starts to smell very strong, remove from heat; it could be burning. When the caramel appears to have thickened considerably and darkened in color, remove from heat.

3. Slowly whisk in the vanilla extract, coconut oil, and sea salt. Let the caramel cool for at least 10 minutes, to thicken up more. Pour the caramel into a small jar and serve with sliced apples. Store any leftover caramel in a sealed jar in the refrigerator for up to 2 weeks.

Perfect Paleo Pancakes

These fluffy pancakes are a great breakfast when you have a nerve-racking day coming up. Whatever uncertainty may lie ahead, you can be sure that breakfast will be special. If you're serving a hungry group, double the recipe!

YIELD: 15 MEDIUM PANCAKES (SF) *option*

Ingredients

4 large eggs

1 cup full-fat coconut milk

¼ cup coconut oil, melted and at room temperature, plus more for greasing the pan

1 Tbsp pure maple syrup*

1 tsp vanilla extract

1 tsp apple cider vinegar

1½ cups blanched almond flour

½ cup arrowroot flour

3 Tbsp coconut flour

½ tsp baking soda

¼ tsp sea salt

Optional toppings: berries, Coconut Whipped Cream (page 100), maple syrup*

 To make this recipe sugar-free, replace the pure maple syrup with monk fruit maple-flavored syrup, or just omit it.

Instructions

1. Heat a large griddle or pan over medium-low heat on the stove, to preheat. I like to use a large cast-iron griddle for best results. Lightly grease the pan with about 1 tablespoon coconut oil.

2. In a large bowl, whisk together the eggs, coconut milk, melted coconut oil, maple syrup, vanilla extract, and apple cider vinegar.

3. In a medium bowl, mix together the almond flour, arrowroot flour, coconut flour, baking soda, and sea salt. Mix the dry ingredients into the wet and stir using a rubber spatula until there are no lumps.

4. Let the batter sit for 5 minutes, to thicken, then give it a brief stir. For each pancake, spoon a scant ¼ cup of batter onto the greased and preheated pan. Position the pancakes at least 2 inches apart from each other, because they will spread.

5. Cook each pancake for approximately 2 minutes on each side, or until it is golden brown and cooked through. Flip them onto a plate and cook the rest of your batter. Note that the second and third batches of pancakes will cook much quicker than the first because the pan is hotter, so monitor them to make sure they're not overcooking on the outside. Serve the pancakes with toppings, if desired.

Tahini Chocolate Chunk Blondies

Originating in the Middle East, tahini is a spread made from ground sesame seeds. It gives these treats an inviting, complex flavor. If you've never tasted tahini before and you're unsure if you'll like it, relish the unknown and give these blondies a try!

YIELD: 9 LARGE OR 16 SMALL BLONDIES

 option

Ingredients

1 large egg

1 cup tahini

¼ cup coconut sugar*

3 Tbsp pure maple syrup*

1 tsp vanilla extract

¾ tsp baking soda

¼ tsp sea salt

½ cup chopped dark chocolate*

½ tsp flaky sea salt (optional)

 To make this recipe sugar-free, replace the coconut sugar with golden monk fruit sweetener, replace the pure maple syrup with monk fruit maple-flavored syrup, and use stevia-sweetened dark chocolate.

Instructions

1. Preheat your oven to 350°F and line the bottom and sides of an 8 x 8-inch baking dish with parchment paper.

2. In a large bowl, whisk together the egg and tahini just until combined. Whisk in the coconut sugar, maple syrup, vanilla extract, baking soda, and sea salt. Do not overmix. Gently fold in the chopped dark chocolate.

3. Scoop the batter evenly into the prepared baking dish. Bake the blondies for 16 to 20 minutes, or until they're golden brown and the center is just cooked through. Sprinkle the top with flaky sea salt, if using.

4. Let the blondies cool for 10 minutes. Slice them into 9 large squares or 16 smaller squares and serve. Store leftovers in an airtight container at room temperature for up to 3 days, or in the refrigerator for up to 2 weeks.

CHAPTER SIX

Be Cozy

Take It Easy

Can you recall the last time you actually felt peaceful and relaxed? How about well rested? For most of us, that means thinking back a really long time. That's alarming!

I tend to overschedule myself. In my freshman year of high school, I signed up for way too many clubs and activities, on top of all the demanding classes. By the end of each day (usually around midnight), I was exhausted. When I woke up early the next morning to do it all over again, I had no energy whatsoever. I was burned out.

I knew that I couldn't keep going like that. I desperately needed to slow down and take care of myself. To allow myself to feel *cozy*—relaxing for its own sake.

Here are some practices I've developed over the past few years that help me be cozy and take care of my body and mind.

Habitual Ritual

No matter how busy we are, it's always possible to take some time to care for ourselves. And contrary to the social media posts of people getting massages and pedicures captioned "self-care," it doesn't have to cost anything.

One of my favorite ways to get cozy is with morning and evening rituals. They take anywhere from five minutes to an hour in total—whatever amount of time I can commit to each day.

MORNING

Morning rituals help us connect with body and mind before going out into the world. Spending some cozy time each morning gets us calm, centered, and ready for whatever comes our way.

Personalize your rituals so they feel right for you and your body. They don't have to be long or difficult. Even five minutes will have a remarkable effect on your day. Here are some morning rituals you can try:

- **Stretch it out.** Before you get out of bed, do a little stretch to wake up your body.

- **Make airplane mode your best friend.** Leave your phone off for the first hour (or more!) of each day. This lets you adjust to the morning without being bombarded by information, and it also leaves more time for taking care of yourself.

- **Have a cup of tea.** I love the calming practice of heating up some water, letting the tea steep, then slowly sipping it.

- **Cook yourself breakfast.** My go-to breakfast is three eggs fried in avocado oil, with avocado slices and greens. I love this combo because it has protein, fat, and veggies to keep me going until lunch. Whatever your favorite is, make it a few times each week. I know it sounds stressful to cook on a hectic morning, but it can be quick, and it's well worth it for how good it makes you feel.

- **Meditate.** Choose from any of the meditations in this book (pages 60, 121, and 148) or do one of your own. Meditating in the morning is both calming and invigorating. You can meditate for three minutes or thirty—whatever you have time for.

EVENING

Do you know that feeling when you take a hot bath or shower and then plop down on your bed after a busy day? It's the pure relief that comes from taking care of yourself. Try setting aside at least a half hour before bed for some therapeutic evening rituals. For example, if you're aiming to go to bed at 11:00 p.m., finish everything you need to do by 10:30 p.m. at the latest and set aside the last half hour just to relax. Better yet, give yourself a full hour. Here are some evening ritual ideas:

◆ **Take a hot bath.** You can spruce up your water with lavender essential oil or Epsom salt for maximum calming vibes. Bathing not only feels relaxing but the heating-then-cooling of our body temperature also helps induce sleep.

◆ **Flow through some yoga poses.** I love getting a good stretch before bed. Bonus: Do the yoga after your bath, when your muscles are warmed up. It feels fantastic.

◆ **Write down your worries.** Sometimes I can't fall asleep for hours because I'm stressing about, well, *everything*. I have begun a practice of writing down all the things I'm worried about in a notebook. Once they're on the page, I realize these things are much more insignificant than they seemed in my head.

◆ **Cuddle up with a good book.** Usually by the end of the day, after reading so many textbooks, I have no desire to read one more page of any book. But I've found that carving out at least fifteen minutes to read a good book, just for pleasure, is the most enjoyable and relaxing way to end my day. (There's nothing better than getting immersed in a good story!)

Sweet Dreams

The worst part of our fast-paced lives is that *we never get enough sleep.* We go around in a permanent state of semi-exhaustion, every day. I didn't used to worry about this sleep deprivation. I mean, successful people supposedly say they get by just fine on four or five hours, right? Our society views lack of sleep as a badge of honor!

Society is making a huge mistake, as I recently learned from reading Dr. Matthew Walker's book *Why We Sleep.* The book is life-changing. Dr. Walker shows that getting enough sleep is way more important than we ever knew. Sleep-deprived people get injured more, perform worse in sports, and score lower on tests. (I can attest to this!

My SAT scores plummeted when I took the test after a bad night's sleep.) On less than five hours of sleep, we are 4.3 times more likely to get in a car accident than with a full night's sleep. We have higher risks of getting cancer, Alzheimer's disease, obesity, and diabetes. Not getting enough sleep also makes us more prone to depression and suicidal thoughts. Sleep deprivation is actually a life-and-death matter.

The flip side, though, is good news: If we *do* start getting enough sleep, our lives can transform. We'll fend off illness better, do better academically, improve athletically, and have better memories. When we finally get enough sleep, we become superheroes.

So how much sleep is "enough"? Dr. Walker says average adults need about eight hours. But teenagers need a lot more: a whopping nine to ten hours every night! That probably sounds ridiculous to you—it seems as though there just aren't enough hours in the day.

But we so badly need the sleep. So I propose a happy medium: *somehow, we must get a minimum of eight hours of sleep, every night.* Our lives depend on it.

Q&A

Q: I would love to get a full night's sleep, but that's just not realistic. How am I supposed to get eight hours, between early school start times, sports practice, and hours of homework?

A: It's doable. I find the most helpful thing to do is to stay off my phone at night. Ever since I've started doing this, my sleep is much stronger. It can be tempting to check Instagram one last time before turning off the light, but don't do it! The blue light from our devices interrupts our melatonin production, which makes it harder to sleep. Plus, all the content we see on our phones stimulates our brains and keeps us from being able to wind down. Try airplane mode at least two hours before bedtime. It works wonders.

It also helps to get as much done as possible before it gets late. That means writing your essay at 7:00 p.m., instead of 1:00 a.m.! We have to be conscious of the time we spend after school lets out, taking advantage of it and not procrastinating our work. This might mean not watching a show or scrolling through social media right after we get home, and doing our assignments first.

Added bonus: Research shows that a full night's sleep improves our test scores more than staying up late cramming does. We retain the information better, and we actually *learn* while we sleep. So coziness really pays off!

MINDFUL MOVEMENT
WRAPPED-IN-BLANKETS STRETCHES

These are perfect when you're feeling sleepy, low energy, or just so warm and cuddly that you can't get out of bed. They feel incredible on the hips and back. But this can also be a pretty intense stretch, so be gentle with yourself!

1. Find a comfortable, soft surface (like your bed), and lie down on your back. On an inhale, bring your knees into your chest.

2. Hug your knees deeper into your chest as you exhale. If it feels good, you can also squeeze your head toward your knees. Repeat this cycle a few times: inhale, soften and release; exhale, curl inward.

3. Release your grasp on your left leg. Bend your left leg, then place your left ankle on top of your right thigh. Your legs should resemble the shape of a triangle.

4. Clasp your hands around your right thigh. Inhale. Exhale, and gently hug your left leg toward your chest, if it feels good. Repeat this cycle a few times: inhale, soften and open; exhale, curl inward.

5. Switch sides: Place your right ankle on top of your left thigh, and clasp your hands around your left thigh. Inhale, soften and open; exhale, curl inward.

Pumpkin Cake Doughnuts

When the weather turns crisp and leaves start falling to the ground, it's time to cozy up inside and bake these doughnuts. Made with pumpkin purée, pumpkin spice, and a pumpkin glaze, they're the ultimate treat for autumn.

YIELD: 10 DOUGHNUTS　　(SF) *option*

Ingredients

DOUGHNUTS

1 cup unsweetened canned pumpkin purée

2 large eggs

⅓ cup pure maple syrup*

¼ cup coconut oil, melted, plus more for greasing

1 cup blanched almond flour

¼ cup coconut flour

¼ cup arrowroot flour

3 tsp pumpkin pie spice

½ tsp baking soda

¼ tsp sea salt

GLAZE

¼ cup coconut cream, from the top of a chilled 13½-ounce can of full-fat coconut milk, melted

2 Tbsp coconut butter, melted

2 Tbsp pure maple syrup*

2 tsp pumpkin pie spice

¼ cup chopped walnuts, for topping (optional)

Instructions

1. Preheat your oven to 350°F and grease 2 doughnut pans with coconut oil.

2. In a large bowl, whisk together the pumpkin purée, eggs, maple syrup, and melted coconut oil until combined. In a medium bowl, whisk together the almond flour, coconut flour, arrowroot flour, pumpkin pie spice, baking soda, and sea salt. Mix the dry ingredients into the wet and stir until the batter is smooth.

3. Pour the batter into a plastic baggie, then snip off the tip of one corner of the bag. Pipe the batter into the doughnut pans, filling each well almost all the way up and not covering the holes. If you don't have a plastic baggie, you can spoon the batter into the pans.

4. Bake the doughnuts for 15 to 18 minutes, or until a toothpick inserted into the center comes out clean. After letting the doughnuts cool for 5 minutes, flip the pan upside down and transfer the doughnuts onto a cooling rack.

5. In a small bowl, stir together all the glaze ingredients until shiny and smooth. Then dunk the smooth side of each doughnut into the glaze and sprinkle with chopped walnuts. Serve. Store leftover doughnuts in an airtight container at room temperature for up to 3 days, or in the refrigerator for up to 1 week.

 To make this recipe sugar-free, replace the pure maple syrup with monk fruit maple-flavored syrup.

N'Oatmeal Raisin Cookies

If every cozy, rainy morning was bottled up and baked into a cookie, it would taste like these n'oatmeal raisin cookies. They're nutty, with warming cinnamon spice. They taste exactly like your childhood oatmeal cookies—just without the oats!

YIELD: 24–26 COOKIES  *option*

Ingredients

6 Tbsp warm water

2 Tbsp ground golden flaxseed

2 cups finely shredded unsweetened coconut

¾ cup pepitas, roughly chopped

½ cup raisins*

½ cup walnuts, roughly chopped

1 cup blanched almond flour

2 Tbsp coconut flour

1 tsp grain-free baking powder

½ tsp ground cinnamon

¼ tsp sea salt

½ cup coconut oil, melted

6 Tbsp pure maple syrup*

 To make this recipe sugar-free, replace the raisins with stevia-sweetened chocolate chips and replace the pure maple syrup with monk fruit maple-flavored syrup.

Instructions

1. Preheat your oven to 350°F and line a cookie sheet with parchment paper.

2. In a small bowl, whisk together the water and ground golden flaxseed to form a flax "egg." Set it aside for 5 minutes, or until a gel forms.

3. In a large bowl, whisk together the shredded coconut, pepitas, raisins, walnuts, almond flour, coconut flour, baking powder, cinnamon, and sea salt. Pour in the coconut oil, maple syrup, and flax "egg." Stir just until combined.

4. Using a 1½-tablespoon cookie scoop or a heaping tablespoon, scoop the dough into balls and place them on the prepared cookie sheet. I usually do 2 batches of baking because not all of the cookies fit on 1 cookie sheet. If the balls start to fall apart, gently squeeze them with your hands. Flatten the cookie dough balls out halfway.

5. Bake the cookies for 12 to 13 minutes, or until they are golden brown and still slightly soft on top. Let them cool on a cookie sheet for about 15 minutes. The longer they cool, the less crumbly they'll become. Store leftovers in an airtight container in the refrigerator for up to 2 weeks.

Superpowered Mocha Latte

Making and sipping this warming drink is the ritual to start your day in a cozy way. The latte is creamy and frothy, but unlike a commercial mocha, it's not a sugar bomb. Instead, it's got healthy fats and protein to help you feel fantastic.

YIELD: SERVES 2    *option*

Ingredients

4 shots of fresh espresso*

1 cup hot water*

½ cup full-fat coconut milk

¼ cup grass-fed collagen peptides**

2 Tbsp raw shelled hemp seeds

2 Tbsp coconut butter

1½ Tbsp cacao powder, plus more for topping

¼ tsp ground cinnamon

8 to 12 drops liquid monk fruit extract or pure liquid stevia extract, to taste

2 Tbsp organic dried rose petals, for topping (optional)

Instructions

1. Place all ingredients (except the rose petals) in a high-speed blender and blend, starting on low. Slowly turn blender speed up to high, continuing to blend until everything is smooth and frothy.

2. Taste it, add more monk fruit extract, if desired, and blend again.

3. Pour into 2 mugs, top with extra cacao powder and rose petals, if using, and serve.

 If you don't have espresso, replace the 4 shots of espresso and 1 cup hot water with 2 cups hot coffee. For a coffee-free option, you could use 2 cups strongly brewed dandelion tea.

**To make this recipe vegan, omit the collagen peptides.

CHAPTER SEVEN
Be Wild

Your Unmodified Self

Try counting how many times a day you alter yourself in some way to please other people.

It happens a lot!

It could be smiling when you're angry or holding back from speaking your mind. I used to stay quiet when my friends were talking politics because I knew they wouldn't agree with my opinions. And whenever I was around a certain boy, I would laugh at his unfunny jokes, because I wanted him to think I was fun and not too serious. We feel a lot of pressure to contort ourselves just to fit in.

We badly need to let go of this pressure and, instead, tap into our wild side. When we're being wild, it means we're *not changing ourselves for other people*. It means embracing our raw and unmodified selves, just the way we are.

Your Wild Self(ie)

It's easy to fall into the self-altering trap every day, but social media makes it *even easier*. With a few taps, we can completely alter our appearance. The formula for getting a lot of likes on Instagram—a heavily posed, sunlit selfie with some retouching help from Facetune—is one of the most toxic examples of the pressure to alter ourselves. When that altered photo gets more likes, filtering and retouching become a reflex.

We need to stop this artificial craziness and start hanging out with our wild selves. A great way is by posting unretouched photos. Once you start doing it, you might notice that you feel better about yourself. An added bonus is that your friends may be motivated to post unaltered photos, too!

Try this approach:

1.   Pose for selfies the way you're feeling. Don't contort your body or face to look a certain way if it doesn't feel natural. If you feel happy, smile! If you feel excited, jump in the air! If you're mad, yell!

2.   Post the photo directly from your camera roll. Don't zoom in and look at every detail of your appearance. Steer clear of smoothing or brightening filters, and don't open any retouching apps.

3.   Write your caption, post the photo, then exit the app. I had a bad habit of refreshing my photos for five minutes after posting them, to see how many likes they got. Now I post and immediately quit the app.

When you post an unretouched photo, you might not like the way you look. That's okay. That discomfort is the feeling of wildness in action!

Q&A

Q: Posting selfies is one thing, but it feels way harder to express my "wild" self in real life. Won't people just judge me if I'm super different than everyone else?

A: You might be surprised how powerful it can be to flex your unmodified self.
Take the example of Sibyl Buck, who braved the cookie-cutter world of fashion modeling in the 1990s. Sibyl is a free spirit who later became a rock musician. She told me that when she was younger, she squelched her vibrant personality to become a model. But she started to feel terrible when she saw that she was part of a toxic culture that was hurting young girls by making them think they should look a certain way.
So Sibyl chopped off most of her hair and dyed the rest bright red. She began embodying different wild aspects of herself each time she walked down

the runway. She might grin at the audience or stick her tongue out at the end of the catwalk, instead of the usual deadpan look. This was all unheard of in the modeling world, so Sibyl worried that designers would stop hiring her.

To her surprise, the opposite happened. She started getting more and more jobs. Her career took off. As it turned out, the industry was not annoyed by Sibyl's wild style. They were intrigued by how bold and confident she was.

This doesn't mean that being wild will always lead to greater success. But we might end up with an unexpected bonus if we own our wild nature—for example, we might make a new, like-minded friend.

Here are some ways you can express your wildness:

- **Dress to express.** If you have a certain style you love, try incorporating it into your daily wardrobe. I love finding inexpensive, unique clothes at a local thrift store that I've never seen anyone else wear.

- **Listen to the music you love most—even if it's unpopular— and share it with others.** I have a thing for Irish folk music. I never used to share that fact with people because, well, it's not super cool. But recently I played my favorite Irish song for someone I had just met and it turned out they liked Irish folk music, too! We hit it off. Who knew?

- **Identify what makes you unique.** Is there something that makes you different? Maybe it's a certain way you speak or how you walk. Whatever might make you stand out, try owning it instead of hiding it. Accentuate it, even!

MINDFUL MOVEMENT
DANCE LIKE WILD

Women in every era and in each culture throughout the world have expressed themselves through dance. When we dance, we reconnect with our roots. Dancing alone is beautiful because it allows us to move through wild feelings without judgment or filter. It pushes our mind out of the way and lets our body express whatever it feels. There are no rules holding us back—we move freely.

Another awesome part of dancing is that it flushes out the lymphatic system, so it can actually help boost our immunity!

1. Choose a place where you can dance alone. It can be in your bedroom or outdoors—anywhere you feel completely comfortable and unselfconscious.

2. Turn on a song that connects with your mood and dance to the music. Or dance in quiet.

3. Express whatever emotions come up through your body. You may find yourself doing the silliest, most absurd moves ever. That's good! You don't have to dance in any particular way. You may have the urge to let out a sound, such as a huge sigh or a shout. Let it flow through you.

Matcha Coconut Milkshake

Matcha is a green tea from Japan that tastes wild and earthy. It adds complexity and depth to this thick, creamy shake.

YIELD: SERVES 2

Ingredients

MILKSHAKE

1¾ cups full-fat coconut milk

1 cup ice

1 avocado, pitted and peeled

2 large handfuls baby spinach

2 Tbsp raw shelled hemp seeds

1½ tsp matcha green tea powder

¼ tsp liquid monk fruit extract or pure liquid stevia extract

COCONUT WHIPPED CREAM

¾ cup coconut cream, from the top of a chilled 13½-ounce can of full-fat coconut milk

Instructions

MILKSHAKE

1. In a high-speed blender, combine all ingredients (except for the coconut whipped cream) and blend until smooth.

2. Taste the milkshake and add a few more drops of monk fruit extract if you would like it to be sweeter.

3. Pour the milkshake into 2 glasses. Top with coconut whipped cream, if desired, and serve.

COCONUT WHIPPED CREAM

1. Scoop the coconut cream into a large bowl. Whip using a stand or hand mixer until thick and fluffy.

Maple Bacon Chocolate Chip Cookies

There's no better way to bring out our wild, unmodified selves than by joining two primal flavors that drive us crazy. How about bacon and chocolate? This power duo creates the most divine cookies.

If you're vegetarian, bake some regular Chocolate Chip Cookies (page 137) instead!

YIELD: 18–20 COOKIES

Ingredients

1¾ cups blanched almond flour

¼ cup arrowroot flour

½ tsp baking soda

¼ tsp sea salt

2 large eggs

⅓ cup liquid bacon grease*

2 Tbsp sustainable palm shortening, melted

¼ cup coconut sugar

¼ cup pure maple syrup

1 tsp vanilla extract

½ cup finely crumbled cooked bacon

½ cup chopped dark chocolate or dark chocolate chips

Instructions

1. In a medium bowl, whisk together the almond flour, arrowroot flour, baking soda, and sea salt. In a small bowl, whisk together the eggs, liquid bacon grease, palm shortening, coconut sugar, maple syrup, and vanilla extract.

2. Stir the wet ingredients into the dry and mix until smooth. Fold in the crumbled bacon and the chopped chocolate, reserving a bit of both for topping. Let the dough chill in the refrigerator for 30 minutes.

3. Preheat your oven to 350°F and line a cookie sheet with parchment paper.

4. Scoop 18 to 20 balls of cookie dough onto the baking sheet using either a 1½-tablespoon cookie scoop or a heaping tablespoon. Place each dough ball at least 2½ inches apart, because they spread. I usually do 2 batches of baking because not all of the cookies fit on 1 cookie sheet. Sprinkle on some extra bacon and chocolate chunks. Don't flatten out the balls.

5. Bake the cookies for 10 minutes, or until crispy on the outside. Allow to cool for 3 minutes, then enjoy. These cookies are best eaten the day they're made, but leftovers may be stored in an airtight container at room temperature for up to 4 days.

 If your bacon didn't yield a full ⅓ cup grease, you can make up the difference with more melted sustainable palm shortening.

Fig and Balsamic Gelato

If I had to choose between gelato and ice cream, I'd pick gelato every time. It's creamier, softer, and silkier! Sadly, it's also usually super high in sugar. Here's an allergy-friendly version that doesn't use eggs, dairy, or refined sugar. The result is a unique flavor combination: sautéed figs and slightly sweet, slightly tart balsamic vinegar glaze.

YIELD: SERVES 5–6    *option*

Ingredients

GELATO

3½ cups full-fat coconut milk

½ cup classic monk fruit sweetener*

2 Tbsp arrowroot flour

2 tsp vanilla extract

FIGS

1 Tbsp coconut oil

1½ cups roughly chopped fresh figs

BALSAMIC DRIZZLE

6 Tbsp balsamic vinegar

¼ cup chopped walnuts (optional)

 If you're not worried about this recipe being low sugar, you can replace the classic monk fruit sweetener with maple sugar.

Instructions

1. Whisk together the gelato ingredients in a saucepan over medium-high heat. Bring the mixture to a simmer, and let it simmer for about 2 minutes, or until the mixture has thickened enough to coat the back of a spoon.

2. Using a spoon, press the mixture through a fine-mesh sieve into a shallow dish. Place it in the freezer to chill, about 30 minutes.

3. Coat a small frying pan with the coconut oil, then add the chopped figs. Bring the pan to medium-high heat and stir the figs as they cook, occasionally mashing the pieces. Cook for about 10 minutes, or until the figs have softened into a jammy consistency. Set aside.

4. Pour the chilled gelato mixture into your ice cream maker and process per manufacturer's instructions. Scoop the gelato into a shallow dish and stir in the cooked figs. Place the dish in the freezer to firm up, about 30 minutes.

5. Pour the balsamic vinegar into a small saucepan over medium-high heat and bring it to a boil. Turn down heat to medium-low and let the balsamic simmer for about 3 to 5 minutes, or until it has thickened to coat the back of a spoon. Remove from heat.

6. Scoop the gelato into small bowls, drizzle with the balsamic reduction, and top with chopped walnuts, if desired. If you're serving the gelato much later, let it thaw for 10 minutes before drizzling with balsamic reduction and serving. Store leftover gelato in an airtight container in the freezer for up to 2 weeks.

BE BRAVE

CHAPTER EIGHT
Be Brave

Deep Diving

When you picture bravery, what do you see? Someone skydiving, rescuing a baby from a fire, or maybe surfing a forty-foot wave?

I talked with professional surfer Bethany Hamilton. She has actually surfed forty-foot waves. Bethany said that to her, being brave isn't about death-defying feats. Instead, it means taking on any hard task—being "willing to try when something may seem really difficult or impossible."

I agree. To me, one of the bravest things is to commit to trying something totally new, then spending some serious time and effort learning it.

I recently signed up for a Tae Kwon Do class. I've always wanted to learn self-defense, so I decided to give myself the challenge. But I was nervous to start, because I'd never tried martial arts in my life, whereas most people in the class had been doing it since the age of five. It was nerve-racking to try kicks and punches for the first time—especially when I spotted one of my classmates watching my form: a four-year-old boy who was, naturally, much better and more experienced than me.

To channel your bravery, I challenge you to take on a new, big endeavor.

Choose Your Challenge

First you need to pick what you want to do. What is something you've always wanted to do or learn but haven't because it seemed too hard? Invest in that activity and make it your new challenge. This activity should excite you, so that you will enjoy diving into it for hours on end.

Here are some ideas to get your creative juices flowing:

- Run a 5K race.

- Learn to paint, then display your work at a homemade art gallery in your bedroom.

- Learn how to knit a pair of slippers.

- Write and record a song.

- Learn a foreign language.

- Learn a musical instrument—and join a group.

- Build a wood table from scratch.

- Audition for your school musical—especially if you've never sung in public.

Now set aside some time and dive in!

Be Number ~~One~~ 5,873!

When you start, you might worry that you won't be good at this new thing. You probably won't! If it's a musical instrument, you'll make some terrible sounds. If it's knitting, you'll end up with a snarled clump of yarn. Sadly, our culture is obsessed with the fairy tale of everyone being awesome right away. We want instant gratification from everything we do. This makes it hard for us to want to try anything new because we worry about how we'll look if we're bad at it. What we forget is that it takes a lot of hard work to get anywhere worthwhile.

This challenge is going to take some time. It could be months and months before your wood table is done or you're able to run a 5K. That is a *good* thing. The patient hard work will help you grow your abilities and build tenacity. You might even find that you have discovered a new passion.

Q&A

Q: I want to learn how to play guitar and be in a band. But a lot of my friends are already really good musicians. Won't it be demoralizing to start so far behind?

A: It's brave to try something new because we're vulnerable when we're total beginners. It can feel embarrassing to be just starting out, playing basic scales while our friends can play actual songs really well. I remember taking a beginner's ballet class with a bunch of girls who were three years younger than me, experienced, and about a foot shorter. I stuck out and felt like a giraffe.

Bethany Hamilton points out that it's always best to try to focus on our own efforts—and avoid comparing ourselves with others. "It's okay to strive to be *your* best," she said. But you don't need to be *the* best.

So when you're starting something new and you're surrounded by more experienced people, try to keep your focus on what *you're* doing. This will help you let go of comparison and embrace your inexperience!

MINDFUL MOVEMENT
WARRIOR FLOW

Building on Warrior II, this movement is a flowing, dance-like sequence of poses that helps us feel strong. It's also great practice for sending power and energy out into the world. After doing this sequence you may feel more confident tackling whatever challenges await you.

1. Stand on any flat, even surface. Place your feet wide apart, but not so wide that you feel unbalanced.

2. Turn your right leg out to the right side, perpendicular to your left foot. Now turn your left toes slightly in to the right. On an inhale, press your feet into the floor. Lift both arms out to the side, parallel to the ground. On an exhale, bend your right leg. Take a few breaths here in Warrior II.

3. Leave your right leg bent. On an inhale, lift your right arm over your head as you bend to the left at the waist. Exhale. Make sure you keep opening your right knee to the right as you turn your torso to the left. Feel a stretch in your waist on your right side and in your left hip. Take a few deep breaths here in Reverse Warrior.

4. On an inhale, extend your right arm even farther over your head. On an exhale, uncurl yourself and come back into Warrior II.

5. Leave your right leg bent. On an inhale, draw your left arm up and over your head, bending to the right at the waist. Gently rest your right forearm on your right thigh. Reach your left arm even farther to the right, to stretch your waist on your left side. Take a few deep breaths here.

6. Inhale. When you exhale, lift your left arm back, parallel to the ground, for Warrior II. Turn your toes back to center. Turn your left leg out and repeat this sequence on your left side.

Raw Mocha Fudge Cake

We often feel guilty when indulging in "rich" treats. Let's get rid of that guilt, once and for all. Make, eat, and thoroughly enjoy this creamy chocolate dessert. Be brave and dare to indulge!

YIELD: SERVES 8    *option*

Ingredients

CRUST

1¼ cups blanched almond flour

3 Tbsp coconut oil, melted, plus more for greasing

1 Tbsp pure maple syrup*

FILLING

1½ cups roasted unsalted cashews or cashew pieces

¼ cup coconut oil

1 cup full-fat coconut milk

¼ cup pure maple syrup*

½ cup cacao powder

1 Tbsp espresso powder

¼ tsp sea salt

Coconut Whipped Cream (page 100), for topping (optional)

Instructions

CRUST

1. Grease a 6-inch springform cake pan with coconut oil and line the bottom with a circle of parchment paper.

2. Add the crust ingredients to a small bowl and mix with a spoon until a dough forms. Press evenly into the bottom of the cake pan and freeze for 10 minutes.

FILLING

1. Place the cashews and coconut oil in a food processor or high-speed blender. Blend until smooth. Add the rest of the filling ingredients and blend until the mixture is completely creamy.

2. Pour the filling into the frozen crust. Cover the cake pan lightly with tin foil and freeze for 1 hour.

3. Slice the cake into 8 slices. Serve with coconut whipped cream, if desired. Store leftovers in an airtight container in the refrigerator for up to 1 week, or in the freezer for up to 1 month.

 To make this recipe sugar-free, replace the pure maple syrup with monk fruit maple-flavored syrup.

Ice Cream Sandwiches

Mastering this recipe is the perfect challenging project. You'll be rewarded for your efforts in the best way possible: creamy vanilla ice cream sandwiched between two crispy chocolate chip cookies.

YIELD: 6 ICE CREAM SANDWICHES

Ingredients

4 large egg yolks

2½ cups full-fat coconut milk

½ cup classic monk fruit sweetener*

2 tsp vanilla extract

¼ tsp sea salt

1 batch Chocolate Chip Cookies (page 137)

 If you're not worried about the recipe being low sugar, you can replace the monk fruit sweetener with maple sugar.

Instructions

1. Place the egg yolks in a medium heatproof bowl and whisk until smooth.

2. In a saucepan over medium heat, combine the coconut milk, monk fruit sweetener, vanilla extract, and sea salt, then whisk to combine. Bring the mixture to a simmer.

3. Using a measuring cup, ladle 1 cup of the heated coconut milk mixture into the bowl of egg yolks, pouring it in *very* slowly while you whisk vigorously. Pour the egg-yolk-and-coconut-milk mixture back into the pan of simmering coconut milk and whisk to combine.

4. Whisk the mixture continuously for about 6 minutes, or until the mixture thickens enough to coat the back of a spoon.

5. Turn off your stove. Place a fine-mesh sieve or cheesecloth over the top of a large heatproof bowl. Pour the custard through the sieve and into the bowl. Discard anything left over in the sieve.

6. Let the custard cool to room temperature, then pour it into a resealable plastic bag and remove all air. Place the plastic bag in a bowl of ice water until chilled, about 10 minutes.

7. Pour the chilled custard into your ice cream maker and process per manufacturer's instructions. Scoop the ice cream into a shallow dish and freeze it for 1 hour, while you make the cookies.

8. Once the cookies have cooled and the ice cream is frozen, cut the ice cream into cookie-sized circles using a cookie cutter. Place each circle of ice cream on top of a cookie, top with another cookie, then place it on a plate and put it in the freezer. Repeat with remaining cookies (you will have some extra).

9. Serve the ice cream sandwiches immediately. Store any leftovers in an airtight container in the freezer. Defrost about 10 to 15 minutes prior to serving.

Very Berry Tarts

Part of being brave is diving in and not worrying about everything turning out perfectly. Try making these tarts and don't stress if something goes awry. Just enjoy the ensemble of flaky crust, creamy filling, and mounds of fresh berries.

YIELD: SERVES 12–16

Ingredients

CRUST

2 cups blanched almond flour

1 cup arrowroot flour

¼ tsp sea salt

6 Tbsp coconut oil, melted, plus more for greasing

¼ cup pure maple syrup

CUSTARD

2 cups raw cashews, soaked overnight in 4 cups of water, then rinsed

1 cup full-fat coconut milk

½ cup unsweetened coconut flakes

½ cup fresh lemon juice

2 Tbsp pure maple syrup

1 Tbsp coconut oil

1 tsp vanilla extract

3 cups fresh berries of choice

Instructions

1. Grease two 9-inch springform tart pans with coconut oil and preheat your oven to 350°F.

2. Whisk together the almond flour, arrowroot flour, and sea salt in a large bowl. Stir in the coconut oil and maple syrup. Mix with your hands until a dough forms.

3. Divide the dough in half and press it evenly into the 2 tart pans. Using a fork, poke a few holes into the bottom of each crust. Bake for 12 minutes, or until golden brown. Let them cool for at least 20 minutes.

4. In a high-speed blender, blend together all the custard filling ingredients (except the berries) until thick and creamy. Divide the custard filling evenly between the 2 crusts and spread it out smoothly. Top the tarts with berries of choice, then refrigerate until ready to be served.

5. Slice each tart into 6 to 8 slices and serve. Store leftover tart in an airtight container in the refrigerator for up to 1 week.

BE AFRAID

CHAPTER NINE
Be Afraid

Follow Your Gut

It's Saturday night. A group of friends pulls up at your home to pick you up. You're excited for a night out with them. As you're about to climb into the car, you suddenly get a pit in your stomach. *Weird,* you think. *These are my friends—what do I have to worry about?* Yet you still have a queasy feeling. You shrug it off and get into the car.

Now it's Sunday night. You're preparing for your history presentation the next morning. You have to give a ten-minute speech about ancient Rome in front of the whole class. As you picture looking at all their faces, you get the same queasy feeling in your stomach.

What do these situations have in common? In both, your stomach is sending you a message: beware! Our gut is such a powerful communicator that scientists have dubbed it our "second brain." It contains a network of millions of supersensitive neurons that can detect potentially dangerous situations and send us warning messages. These could be pits in our stomach, goose bumps, or other communications from our bodies.

The question in the moment is, which kind of gut reaction are you having? Is it actual danger that you might not be seeing? Or is it just harmless excitement or nervousness—"butterflies"?

Either way, I try to stay tuned to that gut feeling and figure out what it's telling me. I start by asking myself, *Could I actually be harmed by this situation?* If the answer is yes, I try to take the necessary steps to leave the situation and stay safe. If the answer is no, and there is no danger, then I think, *This is something you can tackle.*

For example, when you are getting into the car with your friends, it might be helpful to think, *I'm not sure of my friend's driving skills, or where this party is. Could I be harmed here?* Your gut may be telling you things you need to know. Maybe you decide to bail on the party.

Face Your Fear

Other times, our "second brain" message may just mean that the situation is awkward, embarrassing, or challenging but not dangerous. Like your history presentation. You will feel embarrassed speaking in front of your class. You might even mess up badly. People might laugh! But you won't be in danger. So when you're feeling queasy the night before, you can take note of your fear, but then start preparing for your talk.

Speaking of speaking, talking to a group is one of the biggest fears for most humans. I know it wasn't easy for me at first. But with practice we can tackle anything—even public speaking! Here are a few steps to help face your fear and give a great presentation:

1. Prepare your talk by writing down the major points on note cards. Now, if you forget what to say, you'll have backup! Practice without the cards as much as possible, so you won't have to look down a lot during the presentation.

2. Practice while holding a pet or stuffed animal. Say the words as if you're talking lovingly to that animal, not delivering a speech to a classroom. This will help you get out of your head and into the flow.

3. Next, practice in front of your parents, siblings, friends, or anybody you trust. This will help you prepare for the big day without feeling too nervous. They will still love you no matter how badly you mess up—maybe even more so!

4. Now is the big day. Go forth knowing that you have practiced a lot and you're ready.

As you go about your day, be aware of any signs that your gut is sending you. You might notice a feeling when you're about to have an uncomfortable conversation with a friend, or experience a big life change. Whatever the situation, fully acknowledge whatever signs come up.

Q&A

Q: What if I don't feel a pit in my stomach in dangerous situations? How can I get in better touch with my second brain?

A: A helpful way to connect with our gut is by doing a body-scan meditation. This gets us in tune with our body, so we can better sense if something feels off in our gut.

10-MINUTE BODY-SCAN MEDITATION

1. Lie down on your bed or the floor. Get as comfortable as possible. You may want to place a cushion under your knees or a small blanket under your head.

2. Close your eyes and take a few deep breaths. How does your body feel? Tense, stressed, peaceful, calm? Just observe.

3. Beginning at the very top of your head, very slowly scan your entire body. Go down your head, neck, shoulders, arms, hands, fingers, chest, rib cage, belly, thighs, calves, ankles, feet, and toes.

4. With each body part, what do you feel? Is there a tingling sensation, tightness, or even pain? You don't need to label anything—just breathe into the sensations.

5. Take one final deep breath in through your nose and out through your mouth.

MINDFUL MOVEMENT
CLIMB A TREE

Climbing trees is still so much fun, at any age. I love the challenge of pushing myself to go higher—and even go out on a limb (literally and figuratively). But sometimes it can be terrifying, when I realize I've gone way too high and have no idea how to get down. However, when I do finally make it down, I feel like a total badass! I know it was worth it, even with the fear. So when you're feeling afraid and want to break through it, give this challenge a try.

1. Find a tree.

2. Climb it.

Buckeye Candies

If you feel scared of baking for the first time, these candies are the perfect place to start. They're simple to make (no oven) and taste like they're right out of an old-fashioned candy shop with their creamy, nutty center and crunchy chocolate shell.

YIELD: 14 CANDIES

EF V SF *option*

Ingredients

1 cup unsalted nut butter of choice

¼ cup blanched almond flour

3 Tbsp pure maple syrup*

2 Tbsp coconut flour

¼ tsp sea salt

½ cup chopped dark chocolate*

*To make the recipe sugar-free, replace the pure maple syrup with monk fruit maple-flavored syrup and use stevia-sweetened dark chocolate.

Instructions

1. In a medium bowl, combine all ingredients except the chocolate. Stir until a dough forms.

2. Roll the dough into 14 balls using a heaping tablespoon, and place them on a plate lined with parchment paper. Freeze the balls for about 30 minutes, or until solid.

3. Place the chocolate in a medium heatproof bowl. Melt by microwaving it in 30-second intervals, stirring the mixture until smooth, or in a double boiler (instructions on page 11).

4. Insert a toothpick into the center of a ball and dunk two-thirds of it in the melted chocolate, making sure to leave an open circle at the top.

5. Place each chocolate-coated buckeye back on the parchment-lined plate. Smooth over the toothpick hole with your fingertip. Repeat with remaining balls.

6. Freeze the plate of buckeyes for about 1 hour, or until they're firm, then serve. Store leftover buckeyes in an airtight container in the refrigerator for up to 1 week, or in the freezer for up to 1 month.

Coconut Cashew Probiotic Yogurt

This recipe never fails to amaze me. Somehow, with just five simple ingredients and no special equipment, we can make a tangy, super-thick, creamy yogurt from scratch. So do not fear! Just follow the instructions closely, and it will be as easy as pie (or . . . yogurt).

YIELD: SERVES 14   *option*

Ingredients

2¾ cups full-fat coconut milk

2 cups roasted unsalted cashews (*not* raw)

2 high-quality probiotic capsules*

1 Tbsp pure maple syrup**

1 pinch sea salt

 Use a high-quality refrigerated brand of probiotic for best results. I use Renew Life 50 billion. Some probiotic brands have an added prebiotic. Don't buy that kind! Added prebiotic can hinder the fermentation.

***To make this recipe sugar-free, omit the maple syrup.*

Instructions

1. Gather the equipment you'll need for this recipe: 1 or 2 large glass jars (such as quart-sized mason jars), boiling water, cheesecloth (or thin dish towels), rubber bands, and an oven that's available for 24 hours.

2. Sterilize your jars by placing them in your sink and slowly running boiling water on their sides and inside. Using gloves or oven mitts, carefully pour out the boiling water from the jars. Let them cool to room temperature on the counter.

3. Add the coconut milk and cashews to a high-speed blender and blend until smooth and creamy. Empty the contents of the 2 probiotic capsules into the blender and discard their casing. Pour in the maple syrup and sea salt, and blend until completely smooth.

4. Pour the yogurt mixture into the sterilized mason jars (if your jar is quite large, the mixture might fit all in one jar). Cover the tops of the jars with cheesecloth. Secure the cheesecloth with rubber bands.

5. Turn on your oven light. Do *not* turn on the oven; the oven light is the only heat the yogurt needs in order to ferment. Put the jars of yogurt into your oven. Let the yogurt ferment with the oven light on and door closed for 16 to 24 hours. After about 16 hours you can briefly open the oven door and taste the yogurt to see if it's tangy enough for your liking. The longer it ferments, the tangier it gets.

6. Remove the jars of yogurt from the oven and place them in the refrigerator for at least 2 hours, to solidify. Serve the yogurt. Store leftovers in a jar in the refrigerator for up to 2 weeks.

Strawberry Frozen Yogurt

The best way to tackle a project such as frozen yogurt is to do it in steps. First, make the Coconut Cashew Probiotic Yogurt. Once you've made that yogurt, this recipe isn't so scary. The result is ridiculously refreshing, creamy, and popping with strawberry flavor! Trust me, it's worth it to take the extra step.

YIELD: SERVES 5–6

Ingredients

1 batch Coconut Cashew Probiotic Yogurt (page 126)

2 cups frozen strawberries

2 Tbsp pure maple syrup (optional)

Instructions

1. Combine the yogurt, frozen strawberries, and maple syrup, if using, in a high-speed blender. Blend the ingredients together until smooth and creamy. It may help to use your blender's tamper, if you have one.

2. If you don't have an ice cream maker, just drink the mixture now, like a milkshake!

3. Pour the mixture into an ice cream maker and process per manufacturer's instructions, until the yogurt is thick like ice cream. Scoop into bowls and serve immediately. Store leftovers in an airtight container in the freezer for up to 1 month. Thaw slightly before serving.

BE JOYFUL

CHAPTER TEN
Be Joyful

This Little Light of Mine

We usually think of joy as the way we feel when something exciting happens—getting a job we really want, having someone we like call us, buying a new phone. But the rush we get from those external things is always temporary.

Actual joy has no expiration date. It doesn't depend on our circumstances. Joy is an internal calm. It's the life force that we always have inside us.

We might be joyful while playing a favorite sport or a musical instrument. Whenever I pick up my guitar and start playing, I feel pure joy. Why? Because joy is derived from being in the present moment. When I strum the guitar, everything else falls away and I'm completely focused on the music. I exist only in that moment, which allows joy to flow through me.

The cool thing is, you don't *have* to be doing something you love in order to feel joy. You can always enter the present moment and become aware of the little flame burning within you. Right now, take a few deep breaths to help you connect with the flame. Then imagine it filling your whole body. That joy will always be with you. No matter what happens in your life—whether you lose money, gain money, feel good, or get sick—joy flows through you all the while.

Help Thy Neighbor

Think of the last time you held a door open for a stranger. How did it make you feel? You probably felt pretty good. That was the joy of helping others in full effect! When we do any act of service, big or small, we focus on someone else's needs. And that is an awesome recipe for joy. Many studies confirm that helping others increases our sense of well-being. If we perform even a small act of kindness each day, we feel more joy in our lives.

The key is being of service for the sake of helping others—not for our own gratification. It's easy to fall into the trap of doing something in hopes of getting recognized in some way. But when we do service solely to help others, we will feel the joy stream through us. That's why anonymous acts of kindness are especially powerful. When we know that nobody will see us, our only motivation is the greater good.

There are endless ways to be of service. No act is too small. Here are a few things you can try:

- Give someone a compliment *not* based on their appearance. ("You really know how to make people feel good! You did such a great job today!")
- Bring a cookie for a friend at school or work.
- Take out the garbage (if it's not already your job).
- Organize a donation drive for a homeless shelter.
- Help a classmate solve a tricky problem (academic or social).
- Volunteer doing something you're passionate about.
- Pick up a piece of trash on the sidewalk.

Hear Her

I reached out to some females of all different ages and asked how they've been of service. Here's what they said:

> *I once babysat a few times a semester so my friend could attend a lab. It was no big deal to me, but I think it helped her feel supported.*

> *I used to go to a homeless shelter to hand out food. The look of appreciation on people's faces made me feel like what I was doing had meaning.*

I sent some of my favorite books from a local bookstore to my friends. I wanted them to know that someone was thinking of them.

At the airport, a young mother with a baby was alone and had so much to handle. She was getting searched at TSA and stressing about missing her flight, so I offered to sit with her baby while she handled everything. She was so thankful.

I saw a girl crying outside a classroom. I made my way over and sat down next to her and held out my hand. She looked up at me with her glossy eyes, took my hand, and held it tightly as if to say "Thank you."

Q&A

Q: I can see being joyful when things are going well. But how can I feel joy when I'm going through a tough time and life is really hard?

A: Joy is not dependent on our circumstances. Still, joy can be hard to connect with when life is challenging. Take it from Nikeh Grey, a journalist who suffers from sickle cell anemia, a blood disease. She told me that sickle cell affects every part of her life, and it's highly unpredictable. "You can be fine," she says, "and literally within five minutes you can be in excruciating pain."

When she's in pain, the only way Nikeh can find joy is to do an activity that snaps her out of her rut—stepping outside and enjoying nature (even if "nature" means the little garden at the hospital), writing down her feelings in a notebook, or going to therapy.

If you're struggling to find joy, try doing something that gets you out of your routine. For me, drawing really helps. You might like to go for a walk or blast your favorite album, if that helps you forget your circumstances for a while. Hold on to that space. Whenever you find yourself frustrated or in pain, remember that feeling and let it fill up your entire body. It's here for you always.

MINDFUL MOVEMENT
RUNNING INTERVALS

When you're feeling lots of energy, let it fuel you to run fast! Afterward, the endorphins will make you feel euphoric. If you're struggling to feel joy, this exercise can also help you. When we run, it breaks us out of our negative thoughts and brings us into the present.

You don't have to be a "runner" to do this! There's no correct speed or distance—just whatever feels like a fun challenge.

1. Find a fairly open place to run that you feel comfortable in, such as a fairly open sidewalk or park. You're going to switch between three different running speeds. It helps to use a stopwatch or timer app if you have one.

2. Start your stopwatch (or just estimate the time). Warm up by walking for 2 minutes.

3. Then begin running at a slow but steady pace, for 30 seconds.

4. Now ramp up your speed so you're putting out a solid effort, for 20 seconds.

5. Last, sprint as fast as you can, for 10 seconds.

6. Repeat this 30-20-10 cycle 4 more times, for a total of 5 minutes.

7. You have completed 1 set. Walk for 2 minutes, to catch your breath. Do as many sets as you want. I like to do it for 20 to 30 minutes total (assuming I can last that long).

Chocolate Chip Cookies

Sometimes simple memories bring us the most joy. The taste of chocolate chip cookies takes me back to playdates with friends when I was little, and slow weekend afternoons at home. When you make these, they can help you create new memories, so every time you bite into a chocolate chip cookie, you'll think back to this joyful moment in time.

YIELD: 16–18 COOKIES (EF) *option* (V) *option*

Ingredients

2 cups blanched almond flour

¼ cup arrowroot flour

½ tsp baking soda

½ tsp sea salt

2 large eggs*

½ cup sustainable palm shortening, melted

½ cup coconut sugar

1 Tbsp vanilla extract

¾ cup chopped dark chocolate or dark chocolate chips

2 tsp flaky sea salt, for topping

 To make this recipe egg-free and vegan, replace the 2 eggs with 2 flax "eggs." To do this, simply stir together 2 Tbsp ground golden flaxseed with 6 Tbsp warm water. Let it sit for 5 minutes to form a gel, then use in the recipe in place of the eggs.

Instructions

1. In a medium bowl, whisk together the almond flour, arrowroot flour, baking soda, and sea salt. In a small bowl, whisk together the eggs, palm shortening, coconut sugar, and vanilla extract.

2. Stir the wet ingredients into the dry and mix until smooth. Fold in the chocolate chips, reserving a few pieces for topping. Cover the bowl with tin foil and chill in the freezer for 30 minutes.

3. Preheat your oven to 350°F and line a cookie sheet with parchment paper.

4. Once the dough is done chilling, scoop 16 to 18 balls of cookie dough onto the baking sheet using either a 1½-tablespoon cookie scoop or a heaping tablespoon. I usually do 2 batches of baking because not all of the cookies fit on 1 cookie sheet. Flatten each dough ball out halfway, then sprinkle on some extra chocolate chunks.

5. Bake the cookies for 12 to 14 minutes, or until they're golden brown on the edges. Sprinkle cookies with flaky sea salt. Let them cool for at least 3 minutes, then enjoy. These cookies are best eaten the day they're made, but leftovers may be stored in an airtight container at room temperature for a up to 4 days.

Magical Unicorn Frappuccino

The original drink that inspired this smoothie has chemicals and a load of sugar. *This one is made with fruits, veggies, protein, and fat that will make your body jump for joy!*

YIELD: SERVES 1

Ingredients

SMOOTHIE

One 3½-ounce packet frozen dragon fruit

¾ cup frozen avocado chunks or 1 avocado, peeled and pitted

¾ cup filtered water

¼ cup full-fat coconut milk

1 serving vanilla protein powder

TOPPING

4½ Tbsp coconut cream, divided, from the top of a chilled 13½-ounce can of full-fat coconut milk

1 tsp honey

¼ tsp blue spirulina powder

Instructions

1. Using a high-speed blender, blend together all the smoothie ingredients until smooth. You may need to use your blender's tamper, if you have one, because the smoothie is thick. Set aside.

2. Stir together 1½ Tbsp coconut cream, the honey, and the blue spirulina in a small bowl. Scoop the mixture into a small plastic baggie, then cut off the tip of one corner of the bag. Drizzle the blue coconut cream on the inside of a large glass, in a zigzag design. Reserve some for drizzling on top.

3. Add the remaining 3 Tbsp coconut cream to small bowl and stir vigorously with fork until it's smooth and fluffy.

4. Pour the smoothie into the glass. Top with the whipped coconut cream and a little more blue drizzle, then serve immediately.

Vanilla Sprinkle Cupcakes

When you get stuck in a negative rut, there's a great way to break out and reset. Baking! Try these fluffy cupcakes with silky frosting, then share with loved ones to connect with your inner flame of joy.

YIELD: 12 CUPCAKES

Ingredients

CUPCAKES

1¼ cups blanched almond flour

¼ cup classic monk fruit sweetener*

¼ cup arrowroot flour

¼ cup coconut flour

1 tsp baking soda

¼ tsp sea salt

5 large eggs

⅓ cup full-fat coconut milk

¼ cup monk fruit maple-flavored syrup*

¼ cup sustainable palm shortening or coconut oil, melted

2½ tsp vanilla extract

2 tsp apple cider vinegar

BUTTERCREAM FROSTING

1¾ cups sustainable palm shortening

½ cup honey

⅓ cup coconut cream, from the top of a chilled 13½-ounce can of full-fat coconut milk

2 Tbsp arrowroot flour

1 tsp vanilla extract

⅛ tsp sea salt

2 Tbsp natural sprinkles (optional; not Paleo)

Instructions

CUPCAKES

1. Preheat your oven to 350°F and line a muffin tin with cupcake liners. (I like to use the natural nonstick variety.)

2. In a medium bowl, whisk together the almond flour, monk fruit sweetener, arrowroot flour, coconut flour, baking soda, and sea salt. In a large bowl, whisk together the eggs, coconut milk, monk fruit syrup, palm shortening, vanilla extract, and apple cider vinegar. Whisk the dry ingredients into the wet and stir using a rubber spatula until the batter has no lumps. Let the batter sit for 10 minutes, to thicken.

3. Pour the batter evenly into the muffin tin. Bake the cupcakes for 20 to 22 minutes, or until golden brown and a toothpick inserted into the center comes out clean. Let the cupcakes cool on a cooling rack until they reach room temperature, about 45 minutes.

BUTTERCREAM FROSTING

1. Scoop the palm shortening into a large bowl. Whip using a handheld mixer or stand mixer until there are no lumps. Add the honey, coconut cream, arrowroot flour, vanilla extract, and sea salt, then whip again.

2. Pipe the frosting onto the cooled cupcakes using a pastry bag fitted with a star tip or a plastic baggie with the tip cut off. Or spread the frosting using an offset spatula. Sprinkle with natural sprinkles and serve. Store cupcakes in an airtight container at room temperature for up to 3 days. Or refrigerate for up to 2 weeks and let them reach room temperature (about 1 hour) before serving.

 If you're not worried about this recipe being low sugar, you can replace the classic monk fruit sweetener with maple sugar and the monk fruit maple-flavored syrup with pure maple syrup or honey.

CHAPTER ELEVEN
Be Clear

Clear Your Mind

Do you ever feel like your brain might burst? Right this minute, my mind is simultaneously processing way too many thoughts:

> *Need to walk the dogs.*
> *Text my friend back.*
> *Tomorrow's physics final.*
> *College applications.*
> *Need to make lunch.*
> *What time do I have to wake up tomorrow?*

It seems as though my mind is always on overload. But I'm not actually getting anything done. Why is this?

It's because our brains aren't meant to hold this much information. Science shows that we can only store a maximum of three or four things at once in our conscious mind, also known as our "working memory." When we hold on to more than this, our brains become like messy rooms—cluttered and full of junk, so we can't find anything. No wonder I feel so overwhelmed and disorganized.

If we want to get stuff done, we need to clear our minds. Here is my favorite way:

1. **Make a list of *everything* that's on your mind.** Actually write it all down on a piece of paper. Just getting thoughts out of your head and onto paper helps relieve stress.

2. **Read over the list.** Cross off the items that are just worries you can't do anything about right now. You'll be surprised how many items disappear! Most of what we worry about is out of our control. For example:

   I should have rehearsed more for that interview yesterday.
   How will my friends like the presentation?
   I'm worried about where I'll get accepted to college.

3. **Store the remaining items somewhere.** You can use a calendar, an app on your phone, or whatever works best for you. I like using a planner because it lets me turn my thoughts into physical lists for each month, week, and day. You can use any tool you want. Your mind will feel much freer!

I Intend

Another way we can be clear is by setting intentions each morning. Intentions are statements for how we would like to go about our day. Unlike a goal, an intention doesn't require any steps to reach a certain objective. It's simply a way to *be*.

Intentions work like magic. They affect our behavior, how our day goes, and even what things "happen" to us. Here's how to get started:

1. Make your intentions at a set time each day, such as right after waking up. Take a deep breath. Notice how you feel. Do you have pain anywhere in your body? What is the first thought that pops into your mind? Is your brain racing with stress or worry? Pay attention to all of it.

2. Ask yourself, *What do I want to bring into this day?* Breathe and listen to your body's answer.

3. Roll over, grab a pen and notebook, and write down three intentions for the day. Be sure to state them all in the affirmative. (For example, "I will practice forgiveness" rather than "I will not hold a grudge.") Here is a sample:

   > *I will be patient with myself.*
   > *I will listen intently to others.*
   > *I will speak out of kindness.*

4. Read over your list. Let your intentions seep in. It might help to read them out loud. When you feel satisfied, seal the practice with another deep breath. Throughout your day, whenever you feel yourself becoming overwhelmed or stressed, think back to those statements.

Q&A

Q: Sometimes it's hard for me to be clear about what I want. Like when a friend invited me to go to a party with her on Friday night. I wasn't sure I wanted to go, because some boys who I don't really like were going to be there. But I said I would go because it felt awkward to say no. How can I make decisions based on what I actually want—and stick with them?

A: It's hard to make decisions in the moment when we feel put on the spot. It helps a lot to get clear on our personal boundaries in advance, before the moment arises. That way, when we're faced with a tough decision, we already know where we stand.

And if you get a question you don't feel comfortable answering in the moment, you can always say, "I'll sleep on it." Saying you will get back to someone is a good way to give yourself more time to respond naturally.

Ask yourself, *What things make me really uncomfortable?* Maybe it's going to certain kinds of parties or wearing certain clothing. *What things am I not yet ready to do?* Maybe it's dating or watching a gruesome movie. It's helpful to have some phrases in our back pocket for when this happens:

> *I don't quite feel ready for that.*
> *I'm not comfortable doing that.*
> *Yeah, I'm not really into that.*
> *Let's do this instead!*

Our values change as we grow older. What you're not comfortable with right now may be fine in a year—or even a month. Start by getting clear with your values at this moment. You can always make changes as you grow and evolve.

The Power of No

The most powerful phrase we can have in our back pocket is *NO*. This tiny word is the best tool for building clear boundaries for ourselves, which help keep us safe.

When I was younger, it was really hard for me to tell people no. I vividly remember one day when I was 13 years old and sitting outside at a café doing some homework. A grown man walked up to me and asked if he could sit at the empty seat while he waited for his drink. I didn't know what to say. The thought of this stranger sitting with me made me feel uncomfortable . . . but I didn't want to make him uncomfortable by telling him no.

"Okay . . ." I responded. He sat right down.

As I tried to work, the man began asking me questions about myself—where I lived, where I went to school. I started lying about the answers because it didn't feel right to tell him these things about myself. Then I realized that if I felt this weird talking to him, I probably shouldn't be. So I mumbled something about having to leave, and awkwardly went to sit inside. After I was inside, I looked out the window and saw the man get up and walk away. He had not been a customer at the café. I felt sick to my stomach.

Immediately afterward, I realized the mistake I had made. I hadn't said no.

I had been so caught up in making a strange man feel comfortable that I overrode my own instincts, my own discomfort. Thinking about this made me really mad. How could I have been so ignorant? That situation could've gotten so much worse! I cursed myself for not saying no when my gut told me it was the right thing to do.

Now that I'm older, I look back at that experience and feel grateful. I was so lucky to have learned about *no* without experiencing any physical harm. And now, I know to always say no in uncomfortable situations.

Sometimes saying no alone isn't enough to keep us safe. Sadly, our society generally teaches males to not pay much attention to a woman's words. Sometimes we might have to just get up and leave or take other physical action. But having *no* always prepared gives us more control over situations than we would otherwise have.

Learning how to use *no* is challenging. Years after that café encounter, I'm still getting used to it. With practice, we can get comfortable with the strong, loud clarity of our voices saying "NO."

MINDFUL MOVEMENT
SEATED MEDITATION

Why is a seated meditation considered a mindful *movement*? Meditation teaches us how to be comfortable and present inside our own head and body. That inner clarity is the foundation of all the mindful movements. So, if you're struggling to feel present with yourself in the moving exercises, practice this meditation for a little while. You can add the physical movement once you're comfortable being seated and still.

Since this exercise is done with eyes closed, get familiar with these instructions before you start. You can also record them (slowly!) and play them back as you do the meditation.

1. Take a seat in a comfortable position, or lie down. (Just not in your bed, or you might fall asleep!) Set a timer for 10 minutes.

2. Close your eyes. Take 2 huge deep breaths: in through your nose, out through your mouth. Now let go of any breath pattern and allow your breath to fall into a natural rhythm.

3. What do you see with your eyes closed? Take a look around the world behind your eyelids. Do you notice brightness, colors, shapes? Don't label what you see, just observe it. Notice all the space inside you, how calm it is here. Know that this place is always available to you, whenever you want it.

4. Take a deep breath in through your nose and out through your mouth. At the end of the exhale, pause for a moment of stillness. Don't anticipate the next breath. Just stay here—still, present.

5. Feel your body on the earth. Notice the openness inside you. Tell yourself, *I am*.

6. Breathe in again, and out. Have another moment of stillness. *I am*. Breathe in for your last breath, then let everything out.

7. Continue to breathe in and out. Every time your mind wanders (which is a lot), just gently come back to the breath. When your timer goes off, take 1 last deep breath, let everything out, and gently open your eyes.

Keep this in mind: A lot of people think they can't meditate because their minds constantly wander. Do not fear! This is normal and part of the process. The key is to keep coming back to the breath, over and over.

Snickerdoodle Cookies

Check out the crisp cinnamon exterior and soft, pillowy interior. The process of mixing the dough, forming it into balls, and rolling them in cinnamon sugar is a great way to chill out when you want to clear your mind.

YIELD: 12 COOKIES   (SF) *option*

Ingredients

1¼ cups blanched almond flour

¼ cup arrowroot flour

1 Tbsp coconut flour

1 Tbsp + 1 tsp ground cinnamon, divided

1 tsp grain-free baking powder

¼ tsp sea salt

1 large egg

⅓ cup pure maple syrup*

¼ cup coconut oil, melted

2 Tbsp coconut sugar*

 To make this recipe sugar-free, replace the maple syrup with monk fruit maple-flavored syrup and coconut sugar with golden monk fruit sweetener.

Instructions

1. Preheat your oven to 350°F and line a cookie sheet with parchment paper.

2. In a large bowl, combine the almond flour, arrowroot flour, coconut flour, 1 tsp cinnamon, baking powder, and sea salt. Whisk to combine. In a medium bowl, combine the egg, maple syrup, and coconut oil. Whisk until smooth. Stir the wet ingredients into the dry and mix until there are no lumps.

3. Cover the bowl of dough with tin foil and place in the freezer to chill for 1 hour.

4. Whisk together the coconut sugar and 1 Tbsp ground cinnamon in a small bowl. Set aside.

5. Using a 1½-tablespoon cookie scoop or heaping tablespoon, scoop the dough into 12 balls. Roll each ball in the bowl of cinnamon sugar and place it on the cookie sheet, then flatten out halfway with the palm of your hand.

6. Bake the cookies for 13 to 15 minutes, or until the center of each cookie is firm to the touch. These cookies are best eaten the day they're made, but leftovers may be stored in an airtight container at room temperature for up to 3 days.

Blueberry N'Oatmeal

Warm and comforting, this tastes just like the classic hot cereal, but without any grains! Instead, we use seeds and coconut to fill us up for a busy day ahead. Taking ten minutes to make this recipe in the morning is a wonderful opportunity to set your intentions for the day.

YIELD: SERVES 1

Ingredients

¾ cup fresh blueberries

¾ cup full-fat coconut milk

¾ cup water

1 serving vanilla protein powder

¼ cup finely shredded unsweetened coconut

2 Tbsp chia seeds

1 Tbsp ground golden flaxseed

1 Tbsp raw shelled hemp seeds

Optional toppings: more fresh blueberries, almond butter, cacao nibs, chopped nuts

 If you're in a time crunch, skip this step and just cook the blueberries with the rest of the n'oatmeal ingredients.

Instructions

1. Pour the fresh blueberries into a small saucepan and set over medium-high heat. Let the blueberries cook for about 8 to 10 minutes, or until they begin releasing their juices and become soft and vibrant in color. Set aside.*

2. While the blueberries cook, pour the coconut milk and water into a separate saucepan and turn to medium-high heat. Once it is hot, whisk in the protein powder, coconut, and seeds. Turn the heat down to medium-low. Cook the mixture for approximately 10 minutes, whisking every 30 seconds, or until it has a thick consistency similar to oatmeal.

3. Pour the n'oatmeal into a bowl, top with the cooked blueberries, add any desired toppings, and serve.

Apple Streusel Muffins

Once there aren't a million things running through your head, you can give the present moment your undivided attention. As you make these spice-filled muffins, focus on each step of preparing yourself nourishing food.

YIELD: 10–12 MUFFINS

Ingredients

MUFFINS

3 large eggs

½ cup unsweetened applesauce

¼ cup coconut oil or sustainable palm shortening, melted

1 cup blanched almond flour

¼ cup golden monk fruit sweetener*

¼ cup arrowroot flour

2 Tbsp coconut flour

2 tsp ground cinnamon

1 tsp baking soda

½ tsp nutmeg

¼ tsp sea salt

1 cup chopped apple, in 1-inch cubes

STREUSEL TOPPING

½ cup blanched almond flour

3 Tbsp golden monk fruit sweetener*

1 tsp ground cinnamon

3 Tbsp sustainable palm shortening, chilled

⅓ cup finely chopped walnuts or pecans

Instructions

1. Preheat your oven to 350°F and line a muffin tin with cupcake liners. (I like to use the natural nonstick variety.)

2. In a medium bowl, whisk together the eggs, applesauce, and coconut oil. In a large bowl, whisk together the almond flour, monk fruit sweetener, arrowroot flour, coconut flour, cinnamon, baking soda, nutmeg, and sea salt.

3. Whisk the wet ingredients into the dry and stir with a rubber spatula just until combined. Let the batter sit for 10 minutes, to thicken, then fold in the chopped apple.

4. Make the streusel topping by combining all ingredients in a medium bowl and mixing them together with your hands until combined. The mixture should form coarse crumbs.

5. Pour the muffin batter evenly into the cupcake liners, filling each nearly all the way up. Sprinkle the streusel topping over the muffins.

6. Bake the muffins for 18 to 20 minutes, or until a toothpick inserted into the center comes out clean. Let them cool for 5 minutes, then serve. Store leftover muffins in an airtight container at room temperature for up to 3 days, or refrigerate for up to 1 week.

 If you're not worried about this recipe being low sugar, you can replace the golden monk fruit sweetener with coconut sugar.

CHAPTER TWELVE
Be Blue

Say "Cheese!"

One day I was walking down the street by myself. All of a sudden, a man shouted at me, "Smile!"

"Come on, how about a smile!" he shouted again. I was alarmed. He made me feel weird and uncomfortable, and I didn't know how to respond. So I ignored him and kept walking.

Later that day, I got to thinking. Why do some strangers believe they can say whatever they want to women? Would a stranger ever tell a man to smile? The more I thought about this, the madder I grew.

Why do so many people expect women to be smiling, anyway? Our society has this notion that if a woman is serious or sad—or just not smiling—she is doing something wrong. So we have learned to mask our unhappiness and put on a positive face.

The truth is, it's not our job to make everyone else feel good. What *is* our job is to embrace the way we're truly feeling. If we're feeling down, that's okay. We can let ourselves be sad, without acting like everything's fine.

Blueness is normal. We're done trying to hide it.

Blue Bayou

A little while ago, my dog Molly died. We'd had her basically my whole life. It was devastating. I missed her so much, and couldn't believe that I'd never see her again. I didn't want to delve into the sadness I was feeling because it was too scary to face. I felt that if I went into my blueness, it would overcome me and I would lose control.

I automatically reached for my phone. I opened Instagram and started scrolling and scrolling, but it only made me feel stale and empty. So I turned on the TV and started watching a show. It took my mind off Molly for a few minutes. But once the credits rolled, I felt worse than before.

So I got up and went for a walk outside. After a few blocks, my emotions started bubbling up. I cried, hard. I let go of control and just let all the tears and sadness out. By the time I got home, I was drained and exhausted—and also a little refreshed. I felt better.

When we're blue, our instinct is to try to avoid the feeling by distracting or numbing ourselves. But that rarely helps. We need to fully *feel* our blueness. Whether we're dealing with a breakup, a failed exam, the state of the world, or a friend being unkind, it usually feels better if we let sadness wash over us.

Q&A

Q: Sometimes I get these big waves of negativity for no apparent reason. It feels like everything is wrong with the world. I don't understand it. Is there something wrong with me?

A: I talked about this with psychologist and author Dr. Lisa Damour. She said that when things feel overwhelming—more than we can handle—we should ask for help from a trustworthy adult or counselor. The negativity you feel could be something serious, which you should talk to somebody else about. There's no shame in asking for help—we all need it.

Other times when we feel blue, it could simply be mood swings, which are totally normal. Dr. Damour explains that there's a biological reason for teenage mood swings. As adolescents, our brains have a fully developed emotion center—but our logical center lags behind, and is not fully developed. So when we have strong feelings, our emotions overwhelm our logic and cause powerful mood swings.

(It's always annoyed me when people say "You're just hormonal." This phrase is used to belittle young women when we're experiencing strong emotions. But it's our brain development—for girls *and* for boys—that makes teens moodier!)

MINDFUL MOVEMENT
BRIDGE POSE

Bridge is a gentle backbend that's perfect for blue moods. Once you have let your emotions wash over you, Bridge will help you feel uplifted and energetic. If you feel any tension in this pose, make sure to listen to your body and adjust your position so it feels good.

1. Find a flat, comfortable surface, such as a yoga mat, towel, or carpet. Lie down on your back with your arms at your sides.

2. Bend your knees and firmly plant your feet on the ground, about a foot away from your tailbone. Walk your feet apart so they're as wide as your hips. Point your toes forward, not outward.

3. Lift your hips off the ground. Picture drawing up your outer hips and letting your inner thighs drop down.

4. Lift your chest toward your chin but keep gentle pressure between your head and the floor to protect your neck. Take some deep breaths.

5. Once you've been in the pose for a few breaths, gently lower your hips to the ground.

6. It's really good for the body to twist after backbends. While still on your back, let both knees fall to the right at the same time, pause, and then let them fall to the left, like windshield wipers. Repeat for a few cycles. Roll to your side and gently push your body back up.

Blueberry Lavender Ice Cream

Some people say, "Don't eat your feelings." I say, "Do it!" When you're feeling blue, eat something blue. This ice cream will do the trick. It's creamy, with bright blueberry flavor and mild notes of honey and lavender.

YIELD: SERVES 8–9   EF V

Ingredients

Two 13½-ounce cans of full-fat coconut milk

1½ cups frozen blueberries

¼ cup maple syrup or honey

4 drops food-grade pure lavender oil

Instructions

1. In a high-speed blender, blend together all the ingredients just until smooth. Pour into your ice cream maker and process per manufacturer's instructions.

2. Scoop the ice cream into a freezer-safe container. Eat right away for a softer consistency or freeze for 45 minutes for a firmer consistency. Store the ice cream in an airtight container in the freezer for up to 2 months. Defrost for 45 minutes prior to serving, or until it reaches a scoopable consistency.

Blueberry Coffee Cake

This cake is bursting with juicy blueberries and covered in a buttery, sweet cinnamon crumble. Try baking it when you're taking a break from social media.

YIELD: SERVES 16

Ingredients

CAKE

½ cup blueberries

¼ cup + 1 Tbsp arrowroot flour, divided

1 cup blanched almond flour

⅓ cup coconut flour

¼ cup golden or classic monk fruit sweetener*

½ tsp baking soda

4 large eggs

⅓ cup full-fat coconut milk

¼ cup sustainable palm shortening or coconut oil, melted

1 Tbsp fresh lemon juice

1 tsp vanilla extract

CRUMBLE TOPPING

⅓ cup blanched almond flour

¼ cup golden monk fruit sweetener*

3 Tbsp arrowroot flour

1 Tbsp ground cinnamon

¼ cup sustainable palm shortening, chilled

1 cup finely chopped walnuts

¼ cup blueberries

Instructions

1. Preheat your oven to 350°F and line an 8 x 8-inch baking dish with parchment paper.

2. In a small bowl, toss together the blueberries and 1 Tbsp arrowroot flour. Set aside.

3. In a large bowl, whisk together the remaining ¼ cup arrowroot flour, almond flour, coconut flour, monk fruit sweetener, and baking soda. In a medium bowl, whisk together the eggs, coconut milk, palm shortening, lemon juice, and vanilla extract. Pour the wet ingredients into the dry and stir until combined.

4. Let the batter sit for 10 minutes, then gently fold in the arrowroot flour–covered blueberries. Pour the batter into the prepared baking dish.

5. For the crumble topping, whisk together the almond flour, monk fruit sweetener, arrowroot flour, and cinnamon in a small bowl. Incorporate the cold palm shortening into the mixture using your fingers, then mix in the walnuts. Sprinkle the topping evenly on top of the batter, then sprinkle on the last ¼ cup blueberries.

6. Bake the coffee cake for 42 to 45 minutes, or until a toothpick inserted in the center comes out clean. Let the cake cool for about 10 minutes, then slice it into 16 squares and serve. Store leftover cake in an airtight container at room temperature for 3 days, or in the refrigerator for up to 1 week.

 If you're not worried about the recipe being low sugar, you can replace the golden monk fruit sweetener with coconut sugar.

Cinnamon Baked Apples

When I'm feeling down, nothing is more comforting than a bowl of warm baked apples. This treat tastes like apple pie filling, but it's so much easier to make. It only requires a few ingredients and five minutes of prep, so you'll be able to dive into the goodness in no time!

YIELD: SERVES 6

Ingredients

6 cups cored and sliced apples (about 5 or 6 large apples)

2 Tbsp pure maple syrup

2 Tbsp fresh lemon juice

1½ Tbsp arrowroot flour

2 tsp ground cinnamon

½ tsp ground ginger

¼ tsp ground nutmeg

Vanilla Ice Cream (optional; page 115)

Instructions

1. Preheat your oven to 350°F.

2. In a large bowl, toss together all the ingredients (except for the ice cream) and mix until combined. Pour the mixture evenly into an 8 x 8-inch baking dish. Cover the dish lightly with tin foil.

3. Bake the apples for 40 minutes, then remove the tin foil and bake, uncovered, for 10 more minutes.

4. Let the apples cool for 5 minutes, then top with ice cream, if desired, and serve. Store leftovers in an airtight container in the refrigerator for up to 5 days. Reheat in the microwave for 1 minute before serving.

CHAPTER THIRTEEN
Be Mad

Fuel for Change

As I'm finalizing this book, massive new protests are erupting around the country in response to America's centuries of racism and oppression of Black people. Many state and local governments are already changing their policies in response. These protests are the ultimate example of people using anger to take action and initiate major change.

Anger can fuel change on a smaller scale as well. In 2019, three girls at a North Carolina school (ages 5, 10, and 14) were fed up with their school's dress code, which forced all girls to wear skirts. The skirts were uncomfortable and restricting. They prohibited girls from sitting cross-legged in class and playing certain games at recess. And their legs got really cold in the winter.

One of the three started a petition for the school to allow girls to wear pants. Despite over a hundred signatures, the petition was taken away by a teacher, never to be seen again. But that didn't stop the girls. They decided to work with the American Civil Liberties Union (ACLU) and sue their school for the right to wear pants. And they won. The unfair rule was struck down, and the case got national coverage.

These examples show us that we can use our anger for positive change. When we join together and take action, it's amazing what we can do.

At the personal level, there are also so many things in everyday life that make us angry and can be changed.

In high school, the teacher in my dance class required all girls to wear makeup for the final performance (which was to be held in our gym, with no audience). The grading system went like this: if we didn't wear makeup, we'd fail the final. This rule didn't sit well with me. I don't normally wear makeup—and I really didn't think it should be part of our grade. I knew that if there were boys in the dance class, she wouldn't expect them to wear makeup. I explained this to the teacher, but she brushed me aside. So I got a group of girls together who agreed that the rule was unfair. We did some research and found out that being graded on our makeup was actually illegal gender discrimination.

The next day after class, we spoke to the dance teacher as a group and told her that the rule was not only sexist, but also illegal. She didn't seem to care. She was annoyed that we were questioning her grading system. After a couple minutes of back-and-forth conversation, she finally said that that if we didn't want to get graded on makeup, one of us would have to stand up in front of the class on the day of the final performance to explain why. I agreed to do it.

On the day of the final, my group showed up bare-faced. I stood in the center of the gym and explained to my thirty classmates all the reasons why my group wasn't wearing makeup. Then I sat down. It was anticlimactic and a little awkward, but it felt so good to know that my friends and I had stood up to authority to take a stance and change the rules, if only for our little group, for one final assignment.

It's good to remember that any rule of a school or business that treats a group differently might be illegal. You can try to resolve the problem by having a dialogue about it or complaining in writing. If they don't respond, you may be able to threaten them with a legal claim, like the girls in North Carolina did. This can get results!

Here are some steps I have used to confront unfair practices:

1. **Identify the problem.** Anything that makes your blood boil and seems unfair is a good candidate for change. Friends can also help clue us in to problems we aren't aware of.

2. **Brainstorm solutions.** How can the problem be solved? How can you use your unique talents and abilities to help fix the issue? Write down your ideas. Ask yourself if this is something you can tackle on your own or if it would be better to work with a group of friends. There's huge power in joining together!

3. **Identify the person who can help fix the problem.** Once you see a solution, seek out a person who's in a position to make it happen. Is it a government official, teacher, product manufacturer, or television station?

4. **Reach out.** Talking directly is usually the most effective tactic. This can include speaking at a city council or school board meeting or calling up a company to talk to its CEO. One-on-one communication is usually best, since it provides optimal clarity.

5. **Clearly describe the problem.** This part is key. You must explain the issue from your point of view and share how it makes you feel. Often, people are not aware of how things impact others.

6. **Offer solutions.** What do you think is the best way to fix the problem? Maybe there is a new approach that can make both sides happy? After saying your piece, let the other person offer solutions as well.

7. **Try, try again.** See if you get any response. Depending on the size of the issue, it may take a while to get the process started. If needed, find a new person who may be able to help. Keep trying. If this tactic doesn't work, you could organize a group meeting or a protest to address it. And even if your efforts don't lead to fixing the problem quite yet, there's huge power in questioning authority and using your anger for good.

Q&A

Q: How do I decide which problems I should try to change?

A: There are so many things that can make us mad—from societal injustices to rude comments. But we can't fix them all at once; there are only so many hours in the day! We need to be able to sustain our energy for the long haul. This means we have to choose which problems we put our effort into right now. When you encounter a problem, check in: Would it feel better to just let this go right now? Or is there an action you can take to help try and fix it—and would that be worth it? This is always a personal question. Listen to your gut.

    If we decide to not take action for now, we still need to fully feel our anger so we can release it. I try to let myself scream, cry, and completely feel the rage. It also sometimes feels great to release it through some deep breathing or singing at the top of my lungs.

MINDFUL MOVEMENT
LION'S BREATH

In order to make change in the world, we have to be comfortable using our voice and being LOUD. Lion's Breath helps us do just that. When we roar like a lion, it moves energy through our chest and throat so we can speak our mind. Plus, it's fun to do!

1. Find a flat, comfortable surface, such as a yoga mat, towel, or carpet. Come onto your hands and knees. Make sure your hips are directly over your knees and your shoulders over your wrists. Let your back be flat.

2. On an inhale, come into "cow": shine your heart forward. Slowly let your bottom ribs drop toward the floor. Release your shoulders away from your ears. You can slightly lift your gaze upward or keep your neck flat to relieve tension. Make sure the back of your neck stays long.

3. On the exhale, come into "cat": push your palms into the earth to round your back in the opposite direction. Start by tucking your tailbone, then curling up your whole spine. Broaden your shoulder blades and breathe into the space there. Let your neck hang, relaxed.

4. On an inhale, come back into cow. Stay in cow as you exhale and let out a fierce "HAAAAA!" Stick your tongue out, look up at your brow, and let your eyes roll back. Try to look as ridiculous as you can for the full effect. Repeat this process for a few cycles, until you feel your chest and throat are open.

Chocolate Hazelnut Spread

When I was growing up, my family never bought Nutella. I tried it for the first time a few years ago at a friend's house. It was love at first taste! But I soon fell out of love when I found out that it had ingredients such as skim milk, palm oil, artificial vanilla flavor, and loads of sugar. Give this recipe a try. It's made with simple, unprocessed foods—and I think it tastes better than the original!

YIELD: 2 CUPS    *option*

Ingredients

1 cup chopped dark chocolate*

3 cups roasted hazelnuts

1 Tbsp pure maple syrup (optional)*

¼ tsp sea salt

 To make the recipe sugar-free, use stevia-sweetened dark chocolate and omit the maple syrup.

Instructions

1. Place the dark chocolate in a medium heatproof bowl. Melt by microwaving in 30-second intervals, stirring the mixture until smooth, or in a double boiler (instructions on page 11).

2. Pour the hazelnuts into a high-speed blender and blend until they form a smooth hazelnut butter. It may help to use your blender's tamper, if you have one.

3. Pour the melted chocolate into the blender, along with the hazelnut butter, and blend until smooth and creamy. Add the maple syrup, if using, and the sea salt. The maple syrup will make the mixture a bit thicker, so blend again until it is smooth.

4. Pour the mixture into a jar and use as desired. It's great on bananas, strawberries, pancakes, ice cream—just about anything! It will keep in a jar at room temperature for up to 1 week.

Luscious Lemon Bars

When you're feeling sour, make these bars. They have a buttery shortbread crust and the dreamiest, creamiest lemon filling. This is my family's all-time favorite recipe!

YIELD: 16 BARS

Ingredients

CRUST

½ cup + 3 Tbsp coconut flour

2 Tbsp arrowroot flour

½ tsp sea salt

¼ cup sustainable palm shortening

¼ cup monk fruit maple-flavored syrup*

1 large egg

1 tsp vanilla extract

FILLING

3 Tbsp arrowroot flour

½ tsp coconut flour

¾ cup fresh lemon juice, strained to remove seeds

½ cup + 2 Tbsp classic monk fruit sweetener*

2 Tbsp fresh lemon zest

4 large eggs

1 large egg yolk

Powdered sweetener (page 24), for topping (optional)

Instructions

1. Preheat your oven to 350°F and line the bottom and sides of an 8 x 8-inch baking dish with parchment paper.

2. To make the crust, combine the coconut flour, arrowroot flour, and sea salt in a medium bowl. Whisk until combined. Add the palm shortening, monk fruit syrup, egg, and vanilla extract, then mix until a dough forms.

3. Press the dough evenly into the bottom of the prepared baking dish. Using a fork, poke a few holes in the dough (for ventilation). Bake the crust for 20 to 22 minutes, or until crisp to the touch and light golden in color.

4. While the crust bakes, make the filling. In a medium bowl, whisk together the arrowroot flour, coconut flour, and a few tablespoons of lemon juice. Add the rest of the lemon juice, along with the monk fruit sweetener, lemon zest, eggs, and egg yolk.

5. When the crust is done baking, remove from the oven and *immediately* pour in the filling while the crust is piping hot. Place the pan back in the oven, then lower the oven temperature to 325°F. Bake for 17 to 21 minutes, or until the very center of the filling is just set and springy to the touch.

6. Let the pan cool on a wire rack for 2 hours to completely set. Slice into 16 squares using a sharp, non-serrated knife. Sprinkle with powdered sweetener, if desired, and serve. Store leftover bars in an airtight container at room temperature for 1 day or in the refrigerator for up to 1 week.

If you're not worried about the recipe being low sugar, you can replace the monk fruit maple-flavored syrup with pure maple syrup and the classic monk fruit sweetener with maple sugar.

Brownie Sea Salt Cookies

Sometimes when you're mad at the world, the best thing is to make a batch of chocolatey cookies. And eat them. These are crispy around the edges, soft and fudgy on the inside, and filled with melty, gooey chocolate.

YIELD: 16–18 COOKIES   *option*

Ingredients

1 cup tahini

2 large eggs

⅓ cup coconut sugar*

¼ cup cacao powder

1 Tbsp pure maple syrup*

½ tsp baking soda

½ tsp sea salt

½ cup dark chocolate chips, plus more for topping*

Flaky sea salt, for topping (optional)

 To make this recipe sugar-free, replace the pure maple syrup with monk fruit maple-flavored syrup and the coconut sugar with golden monk fruit sweetener, and use stevia-sweetened dark chocolate.

Instructions

1. Preheat your oven to 350°F and line a cookie sheet with parchment paper.

2. In a medium bowl, combine all ingredients, except for the chocolate chips. Whisk slowly at first, to beat the eggs. Whisk a bit more vigorously, just until all ingredients are smooth and combined. Gently stir in the chocolate chips using a rubber spatula. Don't overmix the dough.

3. Scoop the dough using a 1½-tablespoon cookie scoop or a very heaping tablespoon and place the dough balls at least 1 inch apart on the cookie sheet. If not all the cookies fit on 1 sheet, bake them in 2 batches. Flatten the balls out a little bit with the palm of your hand.

4. Bake the cookies for 7 to 9 minutes, or until *just* done in the center. Let them cool for 1 minute, then serve. These cookies are best eaten the day they're made, but leftovers may be stored in an airtight container at room temperature for up to 5 days.

CHAPTER FOURTEEN

Be Young

Flipping into Freedom

I was at a birthday party on the beach when I met a woman with the most unique personality I've ever encountered. Although she was in her twenties, she seemed like a young child. She did cartwheels across the sand. She belted out show tunes. Most amazingly, she didn't seem to notice or care what other people thought about her. Her energy was so incredible and infectious that I began to sing along with her. I couldn't stop wondering, *Who is this?*

As it turned out, she was Haley Lu Richardson, a deep and fascinating person. She's also a successful, hardworking actress. We talked about a lot of things, including her approach to life. I realized why Haley seems so young. It's not only the cartwheels or songs but also that she's not at all self-conscious—just like a young child.

If you observe preschoolers for a few minutes, you'll notice that they don't hide their feelings. If they feel curious, they ask a question. If they're sad, they cry. If they feel joyful, they skip and jump. They're too young to be self-conscious yet, so they don't worry about how people perceive them.

Haley has learned that life is more fun if she doesn't spend energy worrying about what people think of her. That way she's free to do the things she loves, all out.

Another fantastic benefit of letting go of what other people think is that it has a ripple effect. Haley points out that when we don't feel self-conscious, "it makes other people feel comfortable in themselves." It lets our friends know that they can be goofy and express their young sides, too. That explains why at the beach I was completely comfortable singing show tunes with a bunch of strangers around.

Be Bored

When was the last time you actually had *nothing* to do? It's probably been a very long time. Maybe you were four years old, waiting in line with your mom at the grocery store. While you waited, you hopped up and down, fidgeting, wishing you had something to do.

Now, thanks to technology, we *always* have something to do. If we have to buy groceries, we fill the time standing in line by texting or checking Snapchat. This might appear to be a good thing. No more boredom!

But it's actually really bad. That time we had as kids waiting with nothing to do was a gift, and now we're missing out on it. When we constantly check our phones, it literally prevents us from having new thoughts. I mean, when have you had a great idea about anything while you were scrolling through Instagram? Being "bored" lets us be alone inside our heads, which gives us the space and openness we need for inspiration.

Many successful creative people, such as the acclaimed author Neil Gaiman, swear by having nothing to do when they need inspiration. When a person tells him they want to be a writer, Gaiman says, "Great, get bored." The more time a writer spends sitting quietly, the more ideas they'll get for plots and characters. It's a paradox: the more we do nothing, the more we get done!

To recapture the imagination of young children, I like to take a "boredom break"—an opportunity to stop whatever I'm doing and just *be*. Here's how:

1. The next time there is a lull in your day—in the car, waiting in a line, before bed—resist the urge to reach for your phone. Instead, take a little time to do *absolutely nothing*. Sit or stand still. It will feel awkward. That's good! Breathe deeply. Even a few seconds of this can help open up your mind.

2. You can also do any monotonous, nonstimulating activity. Here are some of my favorites:

    ◆ Lie outside and stare up at the sky.

    ◆ Sit cross-legged and focus on your breath.

    ◆ Go for a quiet walk.

    ◆ Do some stretching.

It doesn't have to take long! And believe it or not, we all have plenty of spare time. We all spend at least an hour (or four . . . or six) each day on our phones. You have plenty of time for a boredom break even if you take just ten or twenty minutes out of your daily phone usage. Getting bored is so vital for our creativity and well-being, we can't afford *not* to do it!

Q&A

Q: I tried being bored. It was impossible to just sit still. After ten seconds, I had to check my phone. How am I supposed to do nothing?

A: Being bored is not only hard, it can actually be scary. Sometimes doing nothing in silence feels like torture. There's a reason for this. Research shows that between our exposure to the hyperspeed of the Internet and our constant phone-checking, we have *physically rewired our brains*. It's now difficult for us to just sit still and not check.

But if we take a little time, we can retrain our brains to be comfortable when we're doing nothing. To help remove the temptation of your phone while you're taking a boredom break, you can:

- **Time it.** Set a timer for twenty or thirty minutes to make sure you have a solid chunk of time with nothing to do. Use something other than your phone, such as an egg timer or a watch, so you're not relying on your phone to keep time!

- **Buddy up.** When you're ready for your break, swap phones with a friend or sibling. That way you won't be able to check your phone because someone else will have it.

- **Break away.** Shut off your phone. Place it in a drawer in your room, or anywhere that's not easily accessible. Go elsewhere for your break, such as outside for a walk. This way you'll have no choice but to be bored.

JUMP ROPE

As kids, we didn't jump rope to get in shape or do our daily cardio. We did it because it was fun. We need to get back to that playful enjoyment of moving our bodies. When you do this exercise, don't worry about getting your heart rate up or doing the perfect workout. Just pretend you're back on the schoolyard and have some fun with it!

1. Jump rope.

Mint Chocolate Cookies

My all-time favorite kind of Girl Scout cookies, hands down, is Thin Mints. It was rough when I went gluten-free and couldn't have them anymore. But now we can all enjoy them again.

YIELD: 28–30 COOKIES

Ingredients

COOKIES

1¾ cups + 2 Tbsp blanched almond flour

½ cup cacao powder

2 Tbsp coconut flour

¼ tsp baking soda

¼ tsp sea salt

⅓ cup sustainable palm shortening, melted

½ cup monk fruit maple-flavored syrup*

1 tsp pure peppermint extract

COATING

1½ cups finely chopped stevia-sweetened dark chocolate*

2 Tbsp sustainable palm shortening

½ tsp pure peppermint extract

If you're not worried about the recipe being low sugar, you can replace the monk fruit maple-flavored syrup with pure maple syrup and replace the stevia-sweetened dark chocolate with regular dark chocolate.

Instructions

1. In a large bowl, whisk together the almond flour, cacao powder, coconut flour, baking soda, and sea salt. In a medium bowl, whisk together the palm shortening, monk fruit syrup, and peppermint extract. Using a rubber spatula, stir the wet ingredients into the dry and mix until smooth. Form the dough into a flat disk, wrap in plastic wrap, and place in the freezer for 30 minutes.

2. Preheat your oven to 350°F and line two cookie sheets with parchment paper.

3. Place a large sheet of parchment paper on a flat surface (such as a chopping block). When the dough is done freezing, place it on the parchment paper, then place another piece of parchment paper on top of the dough.

4. Using a rolling pin, roll out the dough to ⅛-inch thickness. Using a round cookie cutter about 1½ inches in diameter, cut the dough into about 30 disks. Transfer the disks to the parchment-lined cookie sheet.

5. Bake the cookies one sheet at a time. Bake the first sheet for 10 minutes, then rotate and bake for another 10 minutes, or until firm to the touch. Then bake the second sheet the same way. Let the cookies cool on the cookie sheet for 5 minutes, then transfer them to a cooling rack for 15 minutes, to crisp up.

6. Make the coating: melt the chopped chocolate and palm shortening together in a small heatproof bowl in the microwave in 30-second intervals, stirring the mixture until smooth, or in a double boiler (instructions on page 11). Stir in the peppermint extract.

7. Dip the cookies into the chocolate coating one by one, using a fork, then set them back onto the parchment-lined cookie sheet to cool. Place the sheet in the freezer for 15 minutes, then serve. Store cookies in an airtight container in the freezer for up to 2 months.

Chocolate-Glazed Cake Doughnuts

These are right out of a neighborhood doughnut shop, with their fluffy cake, classic chocolate glaze, and colorful sprinkles. They're low in sugar and high in protein. So you can eat wholesome food that makes your body feel good without missing out on a favorite childhood treat.

YIELD: 15 DOUGHNUTS   **SF** *option*

Ingredients

DOUGHNUTS

1½ cups blanched almond flour

¾ cup arrowroot flour

¼ cup coconut flour

1 tsp baking soda

¼ tsp sea salt

5 large eggs

⅔ cup pure maple syrup*

½ cup full-fat coconut milk

¼ cup coconut oil, melted, plus more for greasing

1 tsp vanilla extract

GLAZE

1 cup dark chocolate chips or chopped dark chocolate*

2 Tbsp natural sprinkles (optional; not Paleo)*

 To make this recipe sugar-free, replace the pure maple syrup with monk fruit maple-flavored syrup, use stevia-sweetened dark chocolate, and omit the sprinkles.

Instructions

1. Preheat your oven to 350°F. Lightly grease 3 nonstick doughnut pans with some coconut oil.

2. In a large bowl, whisk together the almond flour, arrowroot flour, coconut flour, baking soda, and sea salt. In a separate large bowl, whisk together the eggs, maple syrup, coconut milk, coconut oil, and vanilla extract. Stir the wet ingredients into the dry and mix just until combined. Let the batter sit for 10 minutes, to thicken up slightly.

3. Pour the batter into a plastic baggie, then snip off the tip of one corner of the bag. Pipe the batter into the doughnut pans, filling each well almost all the way up and not covering the holes. If you don't have a plastic baggie, you can spoon the batter into the pans.

4. Bake for 15 to 17 minutes, or until the doughnuts are golden brown and spring back when touched. Let the doughnuts cool for 10 minutes on a wire rack, then flip the pans upside down, the doughnuts should fall right out. If they stick to the pan, run a butter knife around the edges to release the doughnuts.

5. To make the glaze, melt the chocolate chips in a small heatproof bowl in the microwave in 30-second intervals, stirring the mixture until smooth, or in a double boiler (instructions on page 11).

6. Dip the smooth side of each doughnut into the melted chocolate, then top with sprinkles, if desired. Let them sit for 30 minutes, to let the glaze set a little bit, then serve. If you would like the glaze to be completely solid, let them cool for 2 hours before serving. Store leftover doughnuts in an airtight container at room temperature for up to 5 days.

Gooey Nutty Marshmallow Treats

These bring back memories of eating Rice Krispies Treats, but they're made with far better ingredients. These use homemade honey marshmallows and no grains! While these do not have the same texture as the original (more chewy than crunchy), they evoke the nostalgia—and taste amazing.

YIELD: 24 TREATS

EF

Ingredients

4 cups finely chopped unsweetened coconut flakes

4 cups finely chopped cashews

1 cup water, divided

3 Tbsp unflavored grass-fed gelatin powder

1 cup honey or pure maple syrup

1 Tbsp sustainable palm shortening, melted, plus more for greasing

1 tsp pure vanilla extract

¼ tsp sea salt

Instructions

1. Line the bottom and sides of a 9 x 13-inch baking dish with parchment paper, grease it generously with palm shortening, and set aside.

2. Preheat your oven to 350°F. Pour the coconut evenly onto a cookie sheet. Toast the coconut by letting it bake in the oven for about 10 to 15 minutes, stirring occasionally, until golden brown. Mix the cashews with the coconut on the cookie sheet, then set aside.

3. Whisk together ½ cup water with the gelatin in the large bowl of a stand mixer and set aside. If you don't have a stand mixer, combine them in a large bowl and use a handheld mixer.

4. Whisk together the remaining ½ cup water and the honey in a medium saucepan over medium-high heat. Bring the honey-water mixture to a boil. Let it boil for 12 to 15 minutes, or until it reaches 240°F on a candy thermometer.

5. Turn the mixer containing the gelatin mixture on low. Slowly and carefully pour the hot honey-water mixture down the side of the bowl while the mixer runs. Once it is all in, turn the mixer to medium-high and let it whip for about 8 minutes, or until the mixture becomes very fluffy, white, and triples in volume.

6. Pour in the melted palm shortening, vanilla extract, and sea salt, and whip just until the shortening is combined. Do not overwhip or the marshmallow will start to solidify. Swiftly fold in the toasted coconut and cashews, 1 cup at a time, until everything is combined.

7. Scoop the mixture into the parchment-lined baking dish and smooth it out with a rubber spatula. Do not pack it down. Refrigerate it for at least 4 hours, to set. Using a non-serrated knife, cut into 24 squares and serve. Store in an airtight container in the refrigerator for up to 1 week.

CHAPTER FIFTEEN

Be Grateful

Year-Round Thanksgiving

There is one emotion that has transformed my life: gratitude. As I've worked on feeling grateful more often, it's changed my entire outlook. I've gone from paying attention to negative things to seeing the positive in almost everything. A lot has been written about the magic of this emotion.

Why is gratitude so powerful? To find out, I spoke with Sonja Lyubomirsky, a research psychologist, gratitude expert, and the bestselling author of *The How of Happiness*. Dr. Lyubomirsky told me that gratitude is powerful because it changes the way we think about our lives. When we focus on what we're thankful for, it removes the need for *more*. Instead of wishing our lives were different, gratitude makes us feel content and lets us appreciate what's already here. No matter how hard things are, every life—and every day—has things to appreciate. We can be grateful for the simplest things, like the strong roof over our heads or the blossoming tree outside the window.

Gratitude is also an incredible antidote to comparison. Comparison is a toxic habit that seems to be wired into every human brain. Once, I unconsciously compared my shoes to a classmate's new pair, my phone to a friend's new one, and my math-test grade with a peer's—all in less than a minute.

We *always* end up feeling bad when we compare ourselves or what we have to others. Gratitude offers a way out of that trap. It trains our minds to focus on things for their own sake, rather than how they stack up against others. We can be grateful for the air we breathe, the food we eat, the people who help us—without comparing them to anything else.

The Gratitude Journal

I've always been, let's just say, extremely tuned to other people's emotions. When I was little, I would lie awake every night, often in tears. I would get caught up thinking about all the people I knew and all the problems they were going through. It left me sad and hopeless. So I tried an experiment: I started writing down what I was grateful for, every single night, right before bed. I fell asleep a lot faster.

My gratitude journal also boosted how I felt during the day. I began focusing on the beauty in everything and everyone. Peachy clouds in the evening. A teacher who helped me solve a problem. The morning breeze. The troubling things didn't seem so dire. Because the journaling had such a dramatic effect on my perspective and mood, I've been doing it every night since!

There are many different ways to keep a gratitude journal. I encourage you to try out different ones to see what resonates with you. Here's how to get started:

1. Get a journal and pen you love. This is important! I like writing in simple hardcover lined books. Some prefer a guided notebook, such as the Five-Minute Journal, which is more structured.

2. Write every morning or every night. Some people do it first thing in the morning because it gets their day off to a positive start. I write in my journal at night, right before turning off the light, because it gets me into a calm state before sleep. Or you can do both.

3. List at least three things you're grateful for. It can be *anything* you appreciate—a backpack that carries all your books, the janitor at school or work who keeps the rooms clean, or your loved one for cooking a meal.

4. Bonus: Write down things you appreciate about yourself. It can be something you did that day or a trait you're proud of, such as "I'm grateful that I'm such a loyal friend." This conditions our minds to focus on our own inner beauty, and it will help us talk kindly to ourselves.

Start by writing in your journal every day for two weeks. See how you feel. Once you've gotten in the groove, it won't seem like a chore. It may even become something you look forward to!

If journaling isn't your jam, here are some other ways to express gratitude:

- Write a thankful letter to a loved one. (You don't have to send it.)

- Keep a running list with you of things you feel thankful for. Add to it whenever you want.

- Create a collage of images that make you smile.

- Call up someone you haven't seen in a while and express your appreciation for them. (This one is always amazing!)

Hear Her

As this book goes to press, we're on lockdown with a pandemic and there are protests for justice all around the world. I asked a dozen females what they're grateful for right now. Here's what they said:

Not struggling for food or water.

An able body.

*Having a place
to call home.*

The strength of my ancestors.

*Poetry—it helps me put words to my feelings
when I can't seem to do it on my own.*

My generation and how open we are.

My job.

My kitten.

Being Black, even with everything going on in the world.

Good books to lose myself in.

Q&A

Q: Some days are just really bad. How do I find things to be grateful for in those times?

A: You don't have to limit your gratitude to "good" things. You can be grateful for a frustrating or even scary experience. Every lousy thing that happens has some benefit. It might teach us a valuable lesson, help us grow, or lead to an unexpected silver lining.

Once I wrote down that I was thankful for failing my driving test! Right after the test I was *anything* but grateful. I was frustrated and humiliated, especially after months of practicing and obsessing over the rules of the road. I cried for an hour. (Okay, more like two.) But by bedtime I had calmed down. I came to realize that it's okay to fail, that life always goes on. I was grateful for my failed test teaching me that. Another unexpected bonus of failing my driving test was that I had the opportunity to practice driving a lot more. I got *really* good at left turns at a four-way stop. The second try was a breeze!

MINDFUL MOVEMENT
TREE POSE

Tree pose gives us a special moment to ground our bodies and minds. As we root down into the earth, we can take the opportunity to feel grateful for exactly where we are right now.

1. Find a flat, even surface for this pose. Stand on your right foot for a few seconds, then on your left, to see which side has better balance.

2. Let's say your left foot has better balance, like mine. Place your weight on your left foot. Lift your right foot off the ground for a moment to get used to standing on one foot. It's okay if you're a little wobbly! To help steady yourself, bring your gaze to the ground a few feet ahead of you.

3. Focus on the wobble in your standing ankle. My teacher Sibyl taught me something fascinating about balance: 80 percent of our nerves of proprioception (our ability to know where we are in space) are in our ankles. So when you focus on the wobble there, you give yourself the best shot at noticing right away when you start to lose balance. The key is noticing as soon as possible when you're going out of balance, so you can correct before it knocks you over!

4. Place your right foot on your left inner calf, right above the ankle. Maintain your gaze out in front of you. Stay here until you feel comfortable balancing.

5. Gently pick up your right foot and bring it to your left inner thigh. It's totally normal to lose balance and fall out of the pose here. If so, just begin again.

6. Place your arms in whichever position helps you balance the best. You can bring your palms together at your heart, bend your elbows out at your side, or lift your arms up high.

7. Once you feel balanced here, you can play around with lifting your gaze upward, or even closing your eyes!

8. Gently place your foot down, then repeat the process on the other side.

Banana Nut Pancakes

I am grateful for cooking banana pancakes on slow weekend mornings, a tradition my dad started when I was little. When I make these, I feel calm and present. I want to share that moment of simple gratitude with you. So stay in your pajamas, grab some bananas, and let's make some crunchy banana pancakes.

YIELD: 12 MEDIUM PANCAKES

Ingredients

1 cup mashed banana (from about 2 large bananas), plus one more banana for garnish

4 large eggs

¼ cup coconut oil, melted, plus more for greasing the pan

1 tsp vanilla extract

1 tsp apple cider vinegar (optional, for more fluffiness)

½ cup blanched almond flour

¼ cup coconut flour

¼ cup arrowroot flour

2 tsp grain-free baking powder

1 tsp ground cinnamon

½ cup roughly chopped walnuts, plus more for garnish

Instructions

1. Bring a large griddle or pan to medium-low heat on the stove, to preheat. I like to use a large cast-iron griddle for best results. Lightly grease the pan with about 1 tablespoon coconut oil.

2. In a large bowl, whisk together the mashed banana, eggs, melted coconut oil, vanilla extract, and apple cider vinegar, if using. In a medium bowl, whisk together the almond flour, coconut flour, arrowroot flour, baking powder, and cinnamon. Whisk the dry ingredients into the wet and stir with a rubber spatula just until combined. Let the batter sit for 5 minutes, to thicken. Fold in the chopped walnuts.

3. Scoop the batter onto the preheated griddle using a ¼-cup measuring cup. Position the pancakes at least 2 inches apart from each other, because they will spread. Gently smooth out the batter using the back of a spoon.

4. Cook each pancake for approximately 2 minutes on each side, or until golden brown and cooked through. Flip them onto a plate and cook the rest of your batter. Note that the second and third batches of pancakes will cook much quicker than the first. Serve the pancakes hot with sliced banana and extra chopped walnuts. Store leftovers in an airtight container in the refrigerator for up to 1 week. Reheat on the stove.

Raw Blueberry Cheesecake

It helps to get clear about what we want and eat foods that make our bodies feel good. Luckily we don't have to miss out on really yummy desserts like cheesecake. This one is made from ingredients such as pecans, cashews, coconut, and blueberries. Your eyes will love it, but so will your body!

YIELD: SERVES 8

Ingredients

CRUST

1½ cups roasted pecan pieces

2 Tbsp monk fruit maple-flavored syrup*

1 Tbsp coconut oil, melted

FILLING

2 cups raw cashews or cashew pieces, soaked overnight in 4 cups of water, then rinsed

1 cup freeze-dried blueberries

½ cup coconut cream, from the top of a chilled 13½-ounce can of full-fat coconut milk

2 Tbsp monk fruit maple-flavored syrup*

2 Tbsp fresh lemon juice

2 Tbsp coconut oil, melted

1 cup fresh blueberries

Instructions

CRUST

1. Line the bottom of a 6-inch springform cake pan with a circle of parchment paper and set aside.

2. In a high-speed blender, blend together the crust ingredients just until it forms a doughlike consistency. It might help to use your blender's tamper, if you have one. Do not overblend or it will turn into pecan butter!

3. Press the pecan crust evenly into the bottom of the cake pan and place in the freezer while you prepare the filling.

FILLING

1. Without washing your blender, combine the filling ingredients (except for the fresh blueberries) and blend until completely smooth.

2. Pour the filling onto the frozen crust and top with the fresh blueberries. Place in the freezer for approximately 5 hours, or until it's frozen through.

3. Using a butter knife, gently swipe around the inside of the pan to loosen the cake. Remove the cake from the springform pan. Slice and serve. Store any leftover cake in an airtight container in the freezer for up to 1 month. Thaw for 15 minutes before serving.

 If you're not worried about this recipe being low sugar, you can replace the monk fruit syrup with pure maple syrup.

Chocolate-Dipped Coconut Macaroons

These cookies are crispy, nutty, and dunked in a luscious layer of dark chocolate. You'd never know it, but they're healthy—they're made with pure coconut, which is a great source of saturated fat. Saturated fat, much misunderstood, is actually good for our bodies. It helps keep our hearts, brains, bones, and immune systems strong. So when you dig into one of these cookies, you can thank it for fortifying you!

YIELD: 20–22 COOKIES  *option*

Ingredients

5 large eggs

3 cups unsweetened finely shredded coconut

⅓ cup classic monk fruit sweetener*

1 tsp vanilla extract

¾ tsp almond extract (omit for nut-free)

½ cup stevia-sweetened dark chocolate*

 If you're not worried about this recipe being sugar-free, replace the classic monk fruit sweetener with maple sugar and use regular dark chocolate.

Instructions

1. Preheat your oven to 350°F and line a cookie sheet with parchment paper.

2. Separate the egg yolks from the egg whites (you can find helpful video tutorials for this on the internet). We're only using the egg whites for this recipe, so you can save the yolks for another day. Place the egg whites in the bowl of your stand mixer, or use a large bowl and a handheld mixer. Whip on high just until the egg whites become super fluffy and they form medium peaks when you flip the whisk over.

3. Using a rubber spatula, gently fold in the shredded coconut, monk fruit sweetener, vanilla extract, and almond extract.

4. Pack the dough into 20 to 22 balls using a 1½-tablespoon cookie scoop or heaping tablespoon, and place them on the cookie sheet. If all the balls don't fit on 1 sheet, you can bake them in 2 batches. Bake the macaroons for 18 to 20 minutes, or until golden brown. Allow them to cool for at least 5 minutes.

5. Line a plate with parchment paper and set aside. Place the chocolate in a small heatproof bowl and microwave in 30-second intervals, stirring until smooth, or melt in a double boiler (instructions on page 11). Dip the bottom of each macaroon into the melted chocolate, then drizzle more melted chocolate on top. Place the macaroons on the plate.

6. Refrigerate the chocolate-dipped macaroons until the chocolate is set, about 10 minutes, then serve. Store leftovers in an airtight container at room temperature for up to 4 days.

Acknowledgments

Thank you to Stephanie Beatriz, Dr. Lisa Damour, Maris Degener, Nikeh Grey, Bethany Hamilton, Dr. Sonja Lyubomirsky, Haley Lu Richardson, and Mikaila Ulmer for sharing your valuable time to speak with me and for your incredible advice. Thanks also to my wonderful friends Emma Porter and Morguinn Korbonski for your helpful feedback.

Jameela Jamil, thank you for being my role model and a badass human being. You and your ideas have changed my life.

Sibyl Buck, a million thanks for mentoring me; letting me pick your brain endlessly for the book; teaching me everything that's in here about mindfulness, yoga, and meditation; and for your detailed feedback on the mindful movements.

To my editor, Diana Ventimiglia: You have honored my vision throughout this process. Thank you for believing in this unusual book concept and for taking a chance on me. Thanks also to the Sounds True team for bringing this book to fruition.

To my agent, Leigh Eisenman: Thank you for supporting me and this project since when I was a wee tenth grader. You're truly committed to spreading positive messages to young women.

Sofia Szamosi, you are the world's coolest cousin. Thank you for sharing your creativity through the astounding illustrations and detailed notes on the manuscript.

To my brother, Jackie: Thank you for always cheering me on, for your insightful feedback, and for shooting beautiful photos for the introduction.

To my dad, Adam: Thank you for patiently working with me throughout every step of the writing and editing process, round after round of priceless red ink (which I have grown to love). You also helped me bring all the pieces of this book together while somehow being simultaneously organized and thoughtful.

To my mom, Kelly: Your beautiful photography is what makes this book. It's been such a privilege to work with you and witness your creative force. Oh, and thank you for teaching me almost every piece of advice that's in here!

Notes

ABOUT THE RECIPES

9   Gary Taubes, *The Case Against Sugar* (New York: Alfred A Knopf, 2016).

9   David Perlmutter, *Grain Brain: The Surprising Truth about Wheat, Carbs, and Sugar—Your Brain's Silent Killers* (New York: Little Brown, 2013).

9   Bryan Walsh, "Ending the War on Fat," *Time*, June 12, 2014, time.com/2863227 /ending-the-war-on-fat.

9   Erin Brodwin, "A Professor of Medicine Explains Why Eating Fat Won't Make You Fat—But Sugar Will," *Business Insider*, November 19, 2017, businessinsider .com/eating-fat-wont-make-you-fat-gain-weight-says-doctor-2017-11.

CHAPTER 2: BE BOSSY

31   "Double-Edged Words," *Economist*, February 13, 2016, economist.com /books-and-arts/2016/02/13/double-edged-words.

32   Kieran Snyder, "How to Get Ahead as a Woman in Tech: Interrupt Men," *Slate*, July 23, 2014, slate.com/human-interest/2014/07/study-men-interrupt -women-more-in-tech-workplaces-but-high-ranking-women -learn-to-interrupt.html.

CHAPTER 5: BE UNSURE

70   Eckhart Tolle, *A New Earth* (New York: Penguin, 2005).

CHAPTER 6: BE COZY

84–85 Matthew Walker, *Why We Sleep: Unlocking the Power of Sleep and Dreams* (New York: Scribner, 2017).

CHAPTER 9: BE AFRAID

119 Adam Hadhazy, "Think Twice: How the Gut's 'Second Brain' Influences Mood and Well-Being," *Scientific American*, February 12, 2010, scientificamerican .com/article/gut-second-brain.

CHAPTER 10: BE JOYFUL

132 Shoba Sreenivasan and Linda E. Weinberger, "Why Random Acts of Kindness Matter to Your Well-Being," *Psychology Today*, November 16, 2017, psychologytoday.com/us/blog/emotional-nourishment/201711 /why-random-acts-kindness-matter-your-well-being.

CHAPTER 11: BE CLEAR

143 Clara Moskowitz, "Mind's Limit Found: 4 Things at Once," LiveScience, April 28, 2008, livescience.com/2493-mind-limit-4.html.

CHAPTER 13: BE MAD

169 Gaby Del Valle, "Girls at a North Carolina School Sued for Their Right to Wear Pants—and Won," Vox, April 2, 2019, vox.com/the-goods/2019 /4/2/18292333/charter-day-school-north-carolina-dress-code-lawsuit.

CHAPTER 14: BE YOUNG

182 Nicholas Carr, *The Shallows: What the Internet Is Doing to Our Brains* (New York: W. W. Norton, 2010).

Resources

MINDSET AND SPIRITUALITY

- ***The Power of Now* (Eckhart Tolle)**. Welcome to the "now," or the present moment. This book shows us that being present is the only way to have a joyful, meaningful life.

- ***A New Earth* (Eckhart Tolle)**. Read this and your life will change forever. Following *The Power of Now*, Tolle's second book is even more incredible than the first. It dives into our ego, stress, the "pain-body," fear, anger, and so much more.

- **I Weigh (website and social media)**. Created by Jameela Jamil, I Weigh is a resource for radical inclusivity. Its goal is to connect, empower, and amplify diverse voices. Join the revolution against shame!

- **"The Power of Introverts" (Susan Cain, TED talk)**. Part of embracing all our moods is harnessing our personality type. As an introvert, I always saw my quiet nature as a negative. Cain shows that introversion can actually be a superpower. Whether you're an introvert, an extrovert, or anywhere in between, you'll enjoy this talk about our different personalities and how they function in our society.

HEALTH, FOOD, AND AGRICULTURE

- ***Grain Brain* (David Perlmutter)**. Why are so many people finding out that eating gluten gives them problems? Why are deadly disease rates skyrocketing? This is only the beginning of an amazing health and science book.

- ***The Case Against Sugar* (Gary Taubes)**. This is a great source for the history and science on our sugar consumption and its connection to chronic diseases including obesity, diabetes, Alzheimer's, and some cancers.

- ***Chef's Table* (TV series)**. If you want to get inspired to cook, or just appreciate food more, watch this series. In it, the most inspiring and creative cooks from around the world make revolutionary food.

- ***Salt, Fat, Acid, Heat* (TV series)**. In this show based on her bestselling book, Samin Nosrat travels around the world exploring the four elements to good cooking—you guessed it—salt, fat, acid, and heat.

- ***The Biggest Little Farm* (documentary)**. This exciting documentary follows the creation of a regenerative farm in Southern California. But the story goes beyond one farm; it reveals how drastically we could change our planet and our lives by farming in a biodynamic way.

- **"How to Green the World's Deserts and Reverse Climate Change" (Allan Savory, TED talk)**. Allan Savory opened my eyes to the epidemic of desertification, which is a huge contributor to climate change. Savory explains how raising livestock in the traditional way, which mimics nature, can help reverse climate change.

WORK, SLEEP, AND USING OUR TIME

- ***Deep Work* (Cal Newport)**. Doing deep work is the only way we can get stuff done in our distraction-filled world. Once we hone our ability to focus, we'll see some amazing results.

- ***Why We Sleep* (Matthew Walker)**. This book will freak you out— but we all need to read it. It could literally save our lives.

- ***The Talent Code* (Daniel Coyle)**. Some people are just born prodigies or geniuses, right? Wrong! Using examples like Mozart and Tiger Woods, Coyle shows us that the key to getting great at something is all about long, hard work—and any of us can do it.

About the Author

Sadie Radinsky is a teenage blogger and recipe creator. She has touched the lives of girls and women worldwide with her award-winning website, WholeGirl.com, where she shares Paleo treat recipes and advice for living an empowered life. She has published articles and recipes in national magazines and other platforms, including *Paleo, Shape, Justine, MindBodyGreen,* and *The Primal Kitchen Cookbook.* She interviews nutrition and well-being experts on her podcast. Sadie's goal is to help other young women appreciate themselves, enjoy life, and make friends with food. She lives with her family in the mountains of Los Angeles.

About Sounds True

Sounds True is a multimedia publisher whose mission is to inspire and support personal transformation and spiritual awakening. Founded in 1985 and located in Boulder, Colorado, we work with many of the leading spiritual teachers, thinkers, healers, and visionary artists of our time. We strive with every title to preserve the essential "living wisdom" of the author or artist. It is our goal to create products that not only provide information to a reader or listener but also embody the quality of a wisdom transmission.

For those seeking genuine transformation, Sounds True is your trusted partner. At SoundsTrue.com you will find a wealth of free resources to support your journey, including exclusive weekly audio interviews, free downloads, interactive learning tools, and other special savings on all our titles.

To learn more, please visit SoundsTrue.com/freegifts or call us tollfree at 800.333.9185.